D0402846

PRESENTING

Lois
Duncan

Twayne's United States Authors Series
Young Adult Authors

Patricia J. Campbell, General Editor

TUSAS 635

LOIS DUNCAN
Reprinted by permission of Oscar and Associates, Inc., and the American Library Association

PRESENTING

Lois
Duncan

Cosette Kies

Twayne Publishers • New York
Maxwell Macmillan Canada • *Toronto*
Maxwell Macmillan International • *New York Oxford Singapore Sydney*

Acknowledgment is gratefully made to those publishers and individuals who permitted the use of the following material in copyright: Excerpt beginning "She landed in the molding litter," from *The Terrible Tales of Happy Days at School* by Lois Duncan (Boston: Little, Brown, 1983), p. 11. Reprinted by permission of Little, Brown and Lois Duncan. Excerpt beginning "A child who dreams of horses," from *Horses of Dreamland* (Boston: Little, Brown, 1987), p. 1. (c) 1985 by Lois Duncan. Reprinted by permission of McIntosh & Otis, Inc., and Lois Duncan. Excerpt beginning "It snowed last night," from *Who Killed My Daughter?* by Lois Duncan (New York: Delacorte, 1992), p. 102. (c) 1992 by Lois Duncan. Reprinted by permission of Dell, A Division of Bantam, Doubleday, Dell Publishing Group, Inc., and Lois Duncan. Book covers of *Who Killed My Daughter?*, *Down a Dark Hall*, *Daughters of Eve*, *Killing Mr. Griffin*, *The Twisted Window*, and *Don't Look Behind You*. Reprinted by permission of Delacorte Press, A Division of Bantam, Doubleday, Dell Publishing Group, Inc.

Twayne's United States Authors Series No. 635

Presenting Lois Duncan
Cosette Kies

Twayne Publishers   Maxwell Macmillan Canada, Inc.
Macmillan Publishing Company   1200 Eglinton Avenue East
866 Third Avenue   Suite 200
New York, New York 10022   Don Mills, Ontario M3C 3N1

Library of Congress Cataloging-in-Publication Data

Kies, Cosette N., 1936–
     Presenting Lois Duncan / Cosette Kies.
          p.   cm. — (Twayne's United States authors series ; TUSAS 635)
(Twayne's United States authors series. Young adult authors)
     Includes bibliographical references and index.
     ISBN 0-8057-8221-4
     1. Duncan, Lois, 1934– —Criticism and interpretation.   2. Young
adult fiction, American—History and criticism.   I. Title.
II. Series.   III. Series: Twayne's United States authors series.
Young adult authors.
PS3554.U464Z73   1993
813'.54—dc20   93-36336
                                                            CIP

The paper used in this publication meets the minimum requirements of American National Standard for Information Sciences—Permanence of Paper for Printed Library Materials. ANSI Z3948-1984. ⊚™

10 9 8 7 6 5 4 3 2 1 (hc)
10 9 8 7 6 5 4 3 2 1 (pb)

Printed in the United States of America

Contents

Foreword

The advent of Twayne's Young Adult Author Series in 1985 was a response to the growing stature and value of adolescent literature and the lack of serious critical evaluation of the new genre. The first volume in the series was heralded as marking the coming-of-age of young adult fiction.

The aim of the series is twofold. First, it enables young readers to research the work of their favorite authors, and to see them as real people. Each volume is written in a lively, readable style and attempts to present in an attractive, accessible format a vivid portrait of the author as a person.

Second, the series provides teachers and librarians with insights and background material for promoting and teaching young adult novels. Each of the biocritical studies is a serious literary analysis of one author's work (or one sub-genre within young adult literature), with attention to plot structure, theme, character, setting, and imagery. In addition, many of the series writers delve deeper into the creative writing process by tracking down early drafts or unpublished manuscripts by their subject authors, consulting with their editors or other mentors, and examining influences from literature, film, or social movements.

Many of the contributing authors of the series are among the leading scholars and critics of adolescent literature. Some are even young adult novelists themselves. Most of the studies are based on extensive interviews with the subject author, and each includes an exhaustive study of his or her work. Although the general format is the same, the individual volumes are uniquely shaped by their subjects, and each brings a different perspective to the classroom.

The goal of the series is to produce a succinct but comprehensive study of the life and art of every leading young adult author writing in the United States today. The books trace how that art has been accepted by readers and critics, evaluate its place in the developing field of adolescent literature, and—perhaps most important—inspire a reading and re-reading of this quality fiction that speaks so directly to young people about their life's experiences.

PATRICIA J. CAMPBELL, General Editor

Preface

I first met Lois Duncan through her writing. Only a few years younger than she, as a teenager in rural Wisconsin I was an avid reader of magazines such as *Seventeen* and *Calling All Girls.* Among the stories and articles I read were those by Lois Duncan. As Duncan matured and began to write for an older audience, I came across her stories and poems in periodicals such as *McCall's* and *The Saturday Evening Post.*

As a working librarian I became familiar with her books for teenagers, discussing them with colleagues and adolescents. Whatever we said back then about Duncan's books had faded in my memory, but one thing remains clear—we all enjoyed them, although some were shocked by the more controversial titles, such as *Killing Mr. Griffin* and *Daughters of Eve.* During the 1980s, Lois Duncan became more established as an author, and she spoke frequently at professional conferences where we librarians could form firmer images for ourselves of Duncan the woman and Duncan the author.

I finally met Lois Duncan personally in June 1992, in a branch of the Evanston Public Library, while she was on a promotion tour for her latest book, *Who Killed My Daughter?* The encounter was brief; as she autographed my copy of her book, we spoke of the interview I would be conducting with her, which had been arranged for later in the month at the American Library Association conference in San Francisco.

In San Francisco I attended a reception in Duncan's honor sponsored by her publishers, and a luncheon where she accepted the Margaret A. Edwards Award. Two days later I met with

Duncan in her hotel room for an interview. Her husband, Don Arquette, was also present.

Lois Duncan is physically small. Her short blond hair is graying, and she wears glasses. Her smile is quick; her voice carefully modulated. On each occasion I saw her, she was wearing lovely pieces of turquoise and silver jewelry from the Southwest.

I had prepared written questions for the interview, and Duncan answered them quickly yet thoughtfully. She projects intensity, especially when talking about her daughter Kait's murder. She is firm in her opinions, but her willingness to laugh indicates a good sense of humor. She is a kind and caring person, whose strength, vitality, and courage are evident.

Lois Duncan cooperated fully in the preparation of this book, *Presenting Lois Duncan*. Having obtained her assistance, I hope that the end result is a good one. My apologies to her in advance for any errors I may have made, and my heartfelt thanks for her help.

Others have also assisted in the writing of this book. The series editor, Patty Campbell, has provided her usual firm guidance with charm and good humor. Sylvia Miller at Twayne also provided wonderful editorial expertise. David Gale, formerly at Dell Publishing Company, was very helpful in providing information and assistance. Karen Nelson Houle and her staff at the Kerlan Collection at the University of Minnesota gave generously of their time. Linda Gilbert, in Albuquerque, served as an invaluable local contact for me. My thanks go to all of them.

In my own workplace, individuals who have given me great help include Beverly Balster, Andrea Banicki, Sarah Freegard, David Hagerman, Brenda Sanger, and Larry Zevnik. Thanks are also owed to all who expressed interest and support for the project.

Although it is always satisfying to finish a large writing project of this sort, I feel sadness with the book's completion. It has been enormously gratifying to study one author in depth, to meet and talk with her personally, and feel a degree of personal identification with her. I hope that the readers of this book—teens, librarians, and teachers, especially—will come to know and understand Lois Duncan as I have through the writing of it.

Chronology

1934	Lois Duncan Steinmetz is born on 28 April in Philadelphia, Pennsylvania, first child of Joseph Janney Steinmetz and Lois Duncan Foley, both professional photographers.
1937	Duncan's brother, Bill, is born.
1939	Family settles in Sarasota, Florida.
1947	Duncan's first story is published in *Calling All Girls*.
1952	Duncan graduates from high school.
1952–1953	Attends Duke University.
1953	Marries Joseph ("Buzz") Cardozo, a prelaw graduate of Duke and air force lieutenant.
1954	Daughter Robin Dale born.
1956	Daughter Kerry Elizabeth born.
1957	First story for adults, "Home to Mother," is published in *McCall's* magazine.
1958	First young adult novel, *Debutante Hill*, wins Seventeenth Summer Award and is published by Dodd, Mead.
1960	Son Brett Duncan born.
1962	Duncan and Cardozo divorce.
1962	Duncan moves to Albuquerque, New Mexico.
1966	Marries Donald Arquette, an electrical engineer.

1966   First young adult thriller by Duncan still in print, *Ransom,* published.

1967   Son Donald Wayne Junior born.

1970   Daughter Kaitlyn Clare born.

1971   Duncan begins to teach in the journalism department of the University of New Mexico.

1976   *Summer of Fear* is published.

1977   Duncan receives B.A. from the University of New Mexico.

1978   *Killing Mr. Griffin* is published.

1979   *Daughters of Eve* is published.

1981   *Stranger with My Face* is published.

1982   *Chapters* is published.

1985   *Locked in Time* is published.

1989   *Don't Look Behind You* is published.

         Daughter Kaitlyn murdered.

1992   *Who Killed My Daughter?* is published.

1992   Duncan receives Margaret A. Edwards Award from the American Library Association.

1. Becoming a Writer

Lois Duncan was born into a happy Philadelphia home. Her father, Joseph Steinmetz, and her mother, Lois Duncan Foley Steinmetz, were both noted professional photographers. Lois was the elder of two children. Her brother, Bill, was an early audience for her imaginative stories. In their younger years when they shared a bedroom, Lois would terrify Bill with tales about the Moon Fairy, who would come to tell them that the moon was falling out of the sky and would destroy the earth.[1]

Because of her father's career, the family moved around a great deal when the children were very young. Joseph Steinmetz was internationally recognized for his work and his photographs appeared in the leading magazines of the day. World War II meant many changes for people, especially military families. Lois's father became chief training officer at the Naval School of Photography at Pensacola. The family settled in Florida when Lois was five. Among her father's magazine assignments at this time was an unusual one, photographing the Ringling Brothers, Barnum and Bailey Circus, which wintered in Sarasota. Lois used some of these photographs in a children's book she wrote many years later, *The Circus Comes Home*.

From an early age Lois was a storyteller. Her parents wrote down her stories until she was old enough to pen her own poems

1

and tales. She was remarkably proficient. In kindergarten, Lois was asked to recite a poem she had composed. Her teacher refused to believe the child had written such a sophisticated piece and sent her to stand in the corner as punishment for lying.

Lois's parents encouraged their daughter's creativity. When Lois was ten she started sending her stories to the magazines where she had seen her parents' material published. The first story Lois submitted for publication was called "Fairy in the Woods." The editor of *Ladies' Home Journal* was kind in his personal rejection letter, telling Lois that her story was nice, but the magazine was not interested in stories about the supernatural. He also told her that she should enclose a stamped, self-addressed envelope with her submitted manuscripts. The rejection did not stop Lois; she continued to write and send her stories to magazines. Her first published, although not purchased, work was a poem, "New Mexico Sky," in *New Mexico Magazine* in 1947.

For three years Lois collected rejection slips. One day after school she met a neighbor, MacKinley Kantor, a best-selling author of works such as *Andersonville.*

Lois's parents urged her to show one of her stories to Kantor; his reaction upon reading the piece was, "My dear, this is pure shit!" After Lois's and her mother's initial shock wore off, Kantor gave Lois some tried and true advice. He told her to write about what she knew, rather than imaginary fantasies of adults and their world.[2]

Challenged by Kantor's words, Lois wrote a story based on herself, a plump, shy little girl with braces and glasses who wrote stories about imaginary adventures. The story was purchased and published by *Calling All Girls,* a national magazine for teens. Seeing this success as confirmation of Kantor's advice, Lois continued to write about everyday events based on her own life, and many of the stories and anecdotes sold.

Duncan published under the name "Lois Duncan" from the beginning, to distinguish herself from her mother, who signed herself "Lois Duncan Steinmetz" on her own publications. The only pseudonym Duncan has ever used was "Lois Kerry," on two college romance novels. This was because a publishing tradition of the time considered it unprofitable for authors to publish more than one book per year. Duncan had just received word of winning

Lois Duncan as a young child with her mother, Lois Duncan Foley Stein-metz. *Credit: Joseph Janney Steinmetz*

a competition, which included publication of her novel *Debutante Hill,* when the first of the college romance novels was accepted. Because of an unwritten restriction that existed at the time against an author publishing more than one book a year, Duncan published the romance under the name "Kerry," her second daughter's name. During a brief period in her life, while writing confession stories—highly moralistic stories on spicy topics for pulp magazines—to support her children, Duncan's work was published anonymously.

A good student, Lois did well in her classes, with the exception of home economics, which she failed for not producing the required skirt assignment—having forgotten to thread the needle. She turned this incident into a humorous tale, one which she retells to this day.

During her high school years, Duncan discovered that she had difficulty with visual memory. This problem was particularly embarrassing with regard to other people. Although she tried all sorts of identification tricks to improve her recall, it was not until she took up photography in her twenties that she was able to overcome this problem by focusing on people's facial characteristics.

With adolescence Duncan outgrew her baby fat, the braces came off, and she discovered she was pretty. She maintained an active social life, keeping a diary that no doubt sparked ideas for her later stories and books about teenagers. She purchased a second-hand jeep with some of the money she earned from her writing. A friend of Duncan's during her high school years describes her as determined, someone who pushed herself and others to succeed.[3]

Duncan describes her passage into the teen years. "Most of those past life memories had faded before puberty, as had the promise of genius I had shown as a child. By the time I reached adolescence I was a typical teenage girl with an unremarkable I.Q. and an eye for good-looking boys. The only two things that set me apart from my peers were my driving desire to be published and the fact that I knew with certainty that I would have five children."[4]

The Steinmetzes often traveled as a family to photography assignments all over the country. Duncan must have found these experiences helpful when she took up photography herself. One of the family's location shoots was in New Mexico, later to be Duncan's home for many years.

When she was sixteen Duncan won second prize in *Seventeen* magazine's annual short story contest. The next year she received third prize, and when she was eighteen she was awarded first prize. The story was entitled "Return." Success was not as automatic in high school activities, however, for she was thwarted in her desire to be editor of the newspaper in her senior year. The post always went to a boy.

The Korean War broke out while Duncan was in high school, and young servicemen were sent to the Sarasota area for training. Lois and her girlfriends enjoyed dating these young men, but were bothered by the temporary nature of these romances and the danger the men would face in combat.

After Duncan graduated from high school she went on to college. Her father and mother had graduated from Princeton University and Smith College respectively, and it was assumed that Duncan would also attend a good school, even though she had not

Lois Duncan as a toddler with her pet dog. *Credit: Joseph Janney Steinmetz*

been an exceptional student in high school. She enrolled as a freshman at Duke University in North Carolina. This seemed to be a normal thing for her to do, and she thought it would be helpful preparation for her career as a writer.

At Duke, however, Duncan discovered that communal dorm life was not for her, and although asked to pledge a sorority, she declined. Duncan found her classes interesting, but considered required writing assignments dull. Her few attempts to inject creativity into class papers were not appreciated, such as an essay on *Othello* for a Shakespeare class, which Duncan wrote as if it were a woman's magazine column, entitling it "Can This Marriage Be Saved?" She also missed solitary walks along the beach, where she was used to thinking and plotting stories.

While at Duke, Duncan had the opportunity to take part in extrasensory perception experiments conducted by Dr. J. B. Rhine.

While I was a student at Duke, Dr. Rhine was writing his ESP experiments at that time, and they were using the freshman class as guinea pigs. You could sign up and get extra credit to be in the experiments. So I did, and I went through some of the preliminary experiments and thought it was fascinating. Later on when I was looking for a subject for *A Gift of Magic* I remembered this experiment, so that was the jumping-off point for that book. . . . When I wrote *A Gift of Magic,* I based that part [psychic talents] upon the Dr. Rhine experiments and my own feelings about them at the time.[5]

She did not test as being psychically gifted at that time, and in fact she did not make the first cut for further study.

When Duncan returned home at Christmas break she shared her misgivings about continuing with college with her family. Her parents were sympathetic yet puzzled, and lack of any alternative on what to do at that point in her life led Duncan back to Duke after break. In those days, it was not considered appropriate for young women to live alone, and Duncan felt she was too grown up to stay at home with her parents.

Duncan was in college during the 1950s. In those years it was expected that young women would get married and become wives and mothers. It was not unheard of for a woman to have certain acceptable careers, such as teaching, and even more prestigious ones such as that of a professional writer, but during the 1950s there was a strong societal expectation that the college years were the time for women to find husbands. It was not uncommon for male professors to comment that the coeds were there to get their MRS. degrees.

Romance and Marriage

In the spring semester Duncan started dating a senior in prelaw, an attractive, charming fellow named Joseph ("Buzz") Cardozo. They were married in a few months' time. Duncan's parents were a bit uneasy about the situation, but they hosted a lovely wedding in the Duke University chapel.

Duncan's husband had been in the Reserve Officer Training Corps at Duke University and so was obligated to spend time in the air force. After his brief basic training in Georgia, the young couple was stationed in upstate New York, where they lived in a

Left: Lois Duncan, about age four seated on the back of a boat. Right: Lois Duncan as a young teenager. *Credit: Joseph Janney Steinmetz*

rooming house with a stuffed elk's head on their bedroom wall. Cardozo was athletic and expected his new wife to share his enthusiasm for hiking, mountain climbing, and hunting. These activities were not Duncan's idea of great fun. Cardozo had not made his passion for the outdoor, rugged life plain before marriage. Although Duncan tried to get into the spirit of crossbow hunting and the like, she reacted to skinning and cooking her husband's kill—a rabbit—by vomiting.

The couple left New York when Cardozo was transferred to Livermore, California, for a short period. Duncan described Livermore in her first published short story for adults, "Home to Mother." This tale is about Lee, a military service wife and new mother, far away from her own mother in New Jersey for the first time. Duncan describes the character's first morning in the young family's dilapidated apartment near the California military base:

> Rick was still asleep, a pillow over his face. Lee resisted a nasty impulse to bang something loudly enough to wake him. Instead

she plucked Lynda from her current bed, a blanket wadded between two chairs, and carried her out to the living room to change her diaper. She paused en route to stick a bottle into a pan of water on the stove. The stove was part of the so-called "kitchenette"—a rather fancy name, Lee thought, for a living-room wall turned into a kitchen. The burner did not work, and she cursed it under her breath and moved to another burner.

By the time she had changed Lynda's diaper, plus her nightie and undershirt, which were also soaking, the water had reached a boil. She took the bottle out of it, and Rick appeared in the doorway just in time to see her pour the water into the coffeepot.

"That's the same water you had the bottle in," he said accusingly.

"So?"

"So I don't care to have Lynda's bottle in my coffee water."[6]

The scene continues. Lee does not change the water; Rick refuses to drink the coffee and leaves for work. Lee continues to have a dismal day. One bright spot is a letter and check from her mother inviting Lee to return home whenever she wants. The tale ends, nevertheless, on a typical 1950s note with Lee realizing that she can cope; she loves her little family and realizes, most importantly, that Rick *needs* her.

The story is not purely autobiographical, of course, but the descriptions and emotions ring so true they are surely derived from Duncan's real-life experience.

After publication of "Home to Mother," Duncan received a number of sympathetic letters from women who had also been service wives living in Livermore. One letter, however, was from a high school male friend of Duncan's now in medical school who chided her for writing a fine story with a fake ending (*Chapters*, 208–9).

While living in Livermore, Duncan drafted the basic plot for a book she would later write entitled *Ransom*, a story about a school bus kidnapping. After the book's publication, a busload of school children were indeed kidnapped in nearby Chowchilla. An angry woman accused Duncan's book of having inspired the perpetrators of the crime. Duncan now wonders if perhaps this was a case of precognition on her part, somehow seeing future events.

Cardozo was next stationed in Everett, Washington. The young couple rented a small house there, and Duncan tried to settle down to being an ideal wife. Her husband didn't want her to work outside the home, arguing that she had no marketable skills, so she used her spare time to write. Her efforts were not terribly successful, however. For some reason, Duncan found she could not write during her pregnancy. After the couple's first child, Robin, was born in 1954, Duncan found she could write easily again, including little pieces about preparing to be a good wife for the teen magazines.

Duncan was in her early twenties when Robin was born. She was a loving and attentive young mother, but Cardozo's enthusiasm was short-lived. At last Cardozo's full-time military obligations were over, and the family returned to Florida, so he could attend law school. Another daughter, Kerry, was born there.

The First Novels

By this time Duncan knew that all was not well with her marriage. Her husband did not spend much time at home and had many excuses for not being there. During this time she took up photography as a hobby, finding it another way to express her creativity and provide another source of income; some of her nature photographs were published in magazines. She also worked on writing novels during this period, feeling ready to produce more fully developed fictional works. Two of these early novels were about a college girl who finds romance and maturity: *Love Song for Joyce* and *Promise for Joyce,* published under the pseudonym Lois Kerry. Duncan also worked on her first book aimed at young adults, a wistful story about privileged "debs" and a girl left out, a novel called *Debutante Hill.* She had acquired an agent to help place her work, and Duncan suggested to her that the young adult novel, then called a "junior" novel, be submitted to a national writing contest.

By that time Cardozo had finished law school and was seeking work as an attorney. Their first child, Robin, always sickly, was very ill. Duncan took the child to Duke University Hospital for kidney surgery, which was successful. Although the couple had some income from the government—the G.I. Bill—the medical bills were devastating, and Duncan realized that the money earned from her writing was going to be important in helping the family meet its financial obligations.

That summer Duncan's agent called in great excitement. Duncan's novel *Debutante Hill* had just won the Seventeenth Summer Literary Award. The award included a thousand-dollar prize, publication, as well as profits to be made from sales of the book. Duncan was thrilled. The money would be most welcome, but her pleasure came primarily from knowing she was now a *real author,* a writer of published *books.*

Duncan later described an interesting detail about the acceptance of *Debutante Hill:*

> Few people are born with editorial connections. You have to make your own contacts with editors. One of the simplest ways to accomplish this is to become established with editors in *their* fledgling days. The story I wrote at thirteen sold to a youth publication called *Calling All Girls.* The young woman who pulled it out of the slush pile and passed it on to the editor-in-chief was a college student who was working there as an intern.
>
> At 22, I submitted a young adult novel to the "Seventeenth Summer Literary Contest" (sponsored by Dodd, Mead). Knowing how great the competition was, I had little hope that my manuscript would even be considered.
>
> To my amazement, my book won the contest. Along with my prize money and the contract to publish, I received a handwritten note from one of the judges. "Hooray for you!" she wrote. "The minute I saw your name on that manuscript, I knew this was one submission I was going to read immediately."
>
> Nine years before, this editor, now working with a major publishing company, had been the intern who had "discovered" me at *Calling All Girls.*[7]

Divorce and a New Life

Although Robin's health had improved and Duncan's writing was successful, her marriage continued to flounder. Even the birth of a third child, a son, Brett, could not stop its inevitable end. Duncan discovered that her husband had been unfaithful to her. She moved her family to Albuquerque after her divorce. Duncan explained:

> It was not a nice divorce, and I wanted to start over. My parents, when I was about twelve, had spent the summer with us, including my little brother, in New Mexico while they were doing writing and photos. I was enchanted with New Mexico and remembered it as a beautiful place—a magical place with the red cliffs and the Indians, the changing scenery and the mountains. I had never seen so much magic in my life. My brother was at that point working in New Mexico. He was at Sandia Laboratories. So it gave me one person that I knew in Albuquerque. . . . It seemed like a good place to escape, so I took the three children and moved out there. My brother introduced me to people, including Don [her second husband]. (CK interview)

Duncan continued to write and take care of her three children. There was a need for a steady income since the child support checks had stopped coming, so Duncan got a job in an advertising agency. This description from *When the Bough Breaks* (1973) in the words of the book's heroine surely reflects Duncan's feeling about the job. "I was never trained as an advertising copywriter. In truth, I was never trained for anything at all. I had planned always, of course, that I should have a career in something—a bright, flaming career filled with purpose and excitement—but I had never come to a definite decision as to what this work would be. There had been so many dreams: Kat Jason, lying on her back in the sand, squinting up at the sky—'someday,' she had thought, 'someday'—because one did not have to make up one's mind *yet*."[8]

Duncan found herself so exhausted at the end of the day that she was unable to write. Nevertheless, she did have a windfall, one check for $500 describing her most frightening moment, and another for $1,000 as prize in a Happy Snapshot contest. As she says, "So with my $1,500 I quit that awful job! Well, actually, I got fired. I wasn't very good at it. I would put the wrong postage on the mail, and I was always frantic because the kids were home from school. So when I left that job I was faced with the decision to go out and find another . . . job or freelance at home."[9]

Fortunately, Duncan discovered the confessions market. She was able to derive a fairly predictable income from these stories of love and remorse and still have time to concentrate on other kinds of writing. She had also met the man who would be her second husband, Donald Arquette, an electrical engineer with Sandia National Laboratories. Duncan comments that her fiancé was not thrilled with her writing activities at that time, which included stories such as "I Carry that Dreadful Disease," and "Can He Bear to Touch Me on Our Wedding Night?" They did marry in 1966, however, and Arquette adopted Duncan's three children from her first marriage. Two more children, Donald Junior and Kaitlyn, arrived later to make the family complete. The Arquettes lived in Albuquerque throughout the years their children grew to maturity.

Duncan had never obtained a college degree, having left Duke at the end of her first year to marry Cardozo. She reentered college at the University of New Mexico and received her bachelor's degree with academic honors in 1977. She has taught writing for magazines at that same institution. She was originally invited to teach by the chair of the journalism department at that time, Tony Hillerman, now a noted author of mysteries with southwestern settings. Much of the material Duncan used in her classes is included in her book *How to Write and Sell Your Personal Experiences,* first published in 1979. She has also addressed aspiring authors at writers's conferences.

Duncan has never concentrated her writing efforts on any one type of writing. She started with short stories, poems, and articles, but she has a special love for writing young adult novels. As she stated in an interview for her publishers conducted in conjunction with the publication of *The Twisted Window:*

> My first book was a young adult novel for the simple reason that I was 20 when I wrote it, and young adult subject matter was all I knew about. I was also, by that time, very used to writing for my peers. I had been submitting stories to magazines since I was 10, had made my first sale to a teen publication at 13, and had written for youth magazines, particularly *Seventeen,* throughout my teen years. Now, over 30 years and 30 books later, although I write many other types of books also, I am—

Lois Duncan and her family in 1973. Seated, left to right: Don Arquette, Jr., Donald Arquette, Sr., Lois Duncan, Kaitlyn and Robin Arquette. Standing, left to right: Kerry Arquette and Brett Arquette.

first and foremost—an author of young adult novels, because I love the sensitivity, vulnerability and responsiveness of that age reader.[10]

She continued to write for women's magazines, serving as a contributing editor until 1992 for *Woman's Day,* and recently concentrating on younger children's books. She has always kept in mind MacKinley Kantor's advice about focusing her writing on what she knows. She has written about being a teenager, married life, motherhood, and divorce. Now she is a grandmother and has begun to write for younger children again. In 1982 Duncan published an account of her writing life entitled *Chapters: My Growth as a Writer.* To date, she has written over forty books.

Duncan's stories and books cannot be considered purely autobiographical, for there is a considerable use of imagination in her work. She has often suggested that beginning writers use the "What if . . . ?" technique. One of her early short stories, "Lisa and the Lion," is based on this idea. Lisa, the heroine of the humorous tale, gets herself into a wild predicament, all because she tells a perfect stranger an inventive prefabrication about herself as a lion tamer, rather than the more mundane truth of her housewife existence. Lisa's adventures all stem from the premise, "What if a housewife were to make up a story about her life to a stranger?"[11]

Although Duncan bases her stories on what she knows, she does not write about everything she has experienced. There are two topics she avoids dealing with empathetically from the character's point of view: explicit sex and drug abuse. The first is a subject she says she finds difficult to describe convincingly, although the scenes of lovemaking in *When the Bough Breaks* are not particularly awkward. The second, drug abuse, is a theme that is painful for her, since some of her own children have had problems with drugs. She has written about the perils of drug abuse and drug dealing, particularly in *They Never Came Home,* and she always condemns the use of drugs.

One of Duncan's trademarks is the use of personal details worked into her stories. Those who know her can chuckle over

Left: Lois Duncan at her word processor. Right: Lois Duncan holding her first grandchild, Erin Foley Mahrer.

these inclusions, for they are little jokes for her family and friends. For example, in an early young adult novel, *The Middle Sister* (1960), Duncan includes the following bit from the effusive letter home from the oldest sister: "Gad, what a weekend! Went to the big Delta dance Saturday night with a boy named Bill Steinmetz, sweet, blond and a divine dancer!"[12]

In talking about using real people's names, Duncan explained:

> Occasionally I get stuck and use people's names for fun. When I do that, the characters are not at all based on the real people. I would never do that with real names of relatives. . . . I just stick them in . . . and use them like that in a very casual form. . . . I would never use a real person with their name and physical description and make them a real character in the book. I would be overwhelmed with lawsuits, and it would be very embarrassing for a person to be exposed like that. . . . I've never used anyone in total, but most of my characters are composites. People never recognize themselves because you never see yourself as others

see you. So I guess I felt quite safe in that. On a few occasions I have been caught. . . . I'd be looking for a name for somebody, and a name would come to mind; it'll sound right, and I'd use it. Later I'd discover I named someone I knew. I never did it deliberately—it would be someone I'd known very slightly. In several cases it's been a friend of one of my children. I'd just heard my child mention somebody, and the name stuck, but the person isn't there in my mind. In *Killing Mr. Griffin* this happened with the name of David Ruggles. I realized it later, but then it was too late. He was a friend of my son's. I certainly didn't do it intentionally. (CK interview)

Without doubt, Duncan's family has had a great impact on her writing. Her young adult thriller *Ransom* (retitled *Five Were Missing* when it was first released in paperback) was conceived when her oldest daughter, Robin, asked why she didn't write something exciting for kids her age. Her closeness to her family is evidenced by her book dedications, mostly to family members, and by the characters in her books based on them.

Tragedy Strikes

In the summer of 1989, Duncan experienced a terrible personal tragedy when her youngest child, Kaitlyn, then an eighteen-year-old premed college student, was murdered. As Duncan describes it:

My teenage daughter, Kaitlyn, was murdered this last summer, shot twice through the head while driving home from a girlfriend's house. . . . Kait was a clean cut honor student who wanted to be a doctor. . . .

The months since Kait's death have been very difficult for our family as my husband, our four remaining children, and I have tried to accept the unacceptable. . . .

April, the heroine of my most recent YA [young adult] novel, *Don't Look Behind You,* was modeled on Kait, and was published one month before her death. In that book, April, a teenage girl is chased by a hit man in a Camaro but manages to escape him. According to a witness, Kait's killer chased her down in a Camaro. I cringe when I think how lightheartedly I created the scene.

Lois Duncan and her husband, Donald Arquette, at Thanksgiving dinner, before the murder of their daughter, Kaitlyn.

Added to the overwhelming grief at the loss of my child is a feeling of terrible impotence which undoubtedly stems from my 40 odd years of fiction writing. I'm used to being able to shape stories as I want the[m]. . . . Outside the printed page we do not have this luxury. Everyone's story is programmed to end with goodbye.[13]

Duncan relates the real-life crime with its accompanying horror in her 1992 book *Who Killed My Daughter?* She tells about her struggles to deal with her daughter's violent death, her growing conviction that communication beyond death is possible, and her frustrations at dealing with the Albuquerque Police Department on the investigation of the crime, which is still unsolved.

Determined to find her daughter's killers, Duncan launched a campaign to find those responsible, uncovering many facts related to Kaitlyn's involvement with the dubious activities of her Vietnamese boyfriend. Because of death threats, Duncan and her husband have moved to an undisclosed location until the crime is solved. Duncan hopes the FBI will take over the investigation and solve the mystery of the brutal slaying. She also hopes that needed information will be supplied by readers of the book—information that will help solve the crime.

Part of Duncan's determination to find her daughter's killer has resulted in promotion connected to her book, *Who Killed My Daughter?* Following the book's publication in June 1992, Duncan has talked to many groups. She has also been on national television programs, including *Good Morning America; Larry King Live, Unsolved Mysteries,* and *Sightings.*

An Important Honor

In January 1992, Lois Duncan was chosen to be the fourth recipient of the Margaret A. Edwards Award. This honor is given by the Young Adult Library Services Association of the American Library Association and is sponsored by the *School Library Journal.* Previous winners of the award have been S. E. Hinton, Richard

Peck, and Robert Cormier. The award recognizes writers whose books have given young adults a window through which they can view the world; a window that will help them understand themselves and their role in society.

Duncan's books singled out by the award committee included: *Chapters: My Growth as a Writer, I Know What You Did Last Summer, Killing Mr. Griffin, Ransom, Summer of Fear,* and *The Twisted Window.* Betty Carter, chair of the award committee commented: "In her novels, Lois Duncan allows readers to look through a window at a world that houses many different individuals—the strong, the weak, the kind, the evil, the fortunate, the underprivileged, the arrogant, the submissive, the impatient, the cautious, the cunning, the caring and the indifferent."[14]

At the award presentation on 27 June 1992, Duncan addressed a room full of publishers, authors, friends, and librarians in San Francisco, who gave the author a standing ovation after her acceptance speech. In the speech, Duncan describes her feelings on receiving the award:

> By pure coincidence, my husband and I were in San Antonio celebrating the birth of our first grandson, at exactly the time of the ALA Midwinter Meeting. Also by coincidence, we were at the Convention Center, cruising the exhibit hall, when the selection committee came racing out of their chambers in search of a telephone so they could call me at my home in New Mexico.
>
> I was standing in their path, and they almost ran over me. My husband and one of my editors were right there with me, and we all received the wonderful news together. It was one of the most incredible experiences of my life.
>
> If the Fairy Godmother of Young Adult Story Writers could come to me with her magic wand and offer me my choice of literary achievement awards, the Margaret A. Edwards is the one I would have wished for. The reason that this particular award is so meaningful is that it's given for a *body* of work. It's exciting, of course, to be honored for a single title, but you're always aware that such an award may be a fluke—that the title, the theme, or even the picture on the jacket may have appealed to a particular judge for personal reasons that had little to do with the quality of the book. The flip side of that coin is the even more disturbing

Lois Duncan autographing copies of her new book, *The Twisted Window,*
in 1987.

possibility that the award-winning book is a once-in-a-lifetime
masterpiece and nothing you write in the future is ever going to
measure up to it.

The Margaret A. Edwards Award evokes no such anxiety, because it honors the author for a lifetime of effort. Despite the fact
that some books are better than others, and that certain books—
let's face it—were total disasters, the message that you have
given me today is that it has all balanced out, and that the over-
all quality of my work is deserving of recognition.

I can't think of any message that could be more gratifying.[15]

2. All Sorts of Writing

Duncan enjoys writing different kinds of things for different people and has been successful in a wide range of published materials. She has written articles on many subjects, as well as stories, poems, and books. She has written for all age groups. Best known for her young adult thrillers, she has produced a number of books in other genres throughout her writing career. Her versatility has made good use of her deceptively simple and precise use of language.

Poetry

Duncan has written poetry throughout her life. She has kept all of her written work throughout the years, and examples of her early poetry can be found in *Chapters*. Inspired by her grandchildren, she has written books of poems for young children. She has also worked with her oldest daughter, Robin Arquette, a producer of audiovisual materials, on a series of audio tapes collectively called the Songs of Childhood: "Songs from Dreamland," "Dream Songs from Yesterday," "Our Beautiful Day," and "The Story of Christmas." These tapes are based on poetry written by Duncan with music composed and performed by Arquette.

The poetry is traditional verse, using meter and rhyme. Duncan's views on poetry are probably best expressed by a character named Joyce in one of Duncan's early novels, who goes away to college and writes poetry:

> Not just writing it, she thought, searching for the words she needed. Creating it. You *write* themes and term papers, you just sit down and knock them out sentence after sentence, page after page, until they're done. There's no real creative effort to something like that. But a poem—a poem comes from inside—you have to live with a poem. . . .
>
> It's a good poem, she thought. I know it is. She had known that while she was writing it from the way the words flowed easily through her mind, singing their way through her pen onto the paper, saying simply and perfectly what she wanted them to say. When it was completed, she had read it over with a deep feeling of satisfaction.[1]

Duncan's books of poetry include: *The Birthday Moon* (1989), *From Spring to Spring* (1982), *Horses of Dreamland* (1985), *Songs from Dreamland: Original Lullabies* (1989), and *The Terrible Tales of Happy Days School* (1983).

Opinions about poetry tend to be personal, probably since poetry is an intense, intimate form of written expression. Duncan's poetry, like her other writing, may often appear simple, yet the meanings and thoughts expressed are often deeper than might appear at first glance. Only one of the poetry books, *The Terrible Tales of Happy Days School,* is overtly humorous, written for Duncan's son Donnie and his friends. It tells about various children in a progressive school, such as one about Melissa who refuses to clean her pet cage:

> She landed in the molding litter
> And all the hamsters ran and bit her.
> The gerbils rushed to bite her too,
> And how those little things could chew!
> The child was such an awful mess
> Her mother had to burn her dress.[2]

Most of Duncan's poetry, however, is lyrical in nature. Perhaps one of her most satisfying is *Horses of Dreamland*, which tells of a little girl's dream of a fantasy horse ride:

> A child who dreams of horses
> Flies fast and far at night
> And travels miles of moon-trail
> Before the sky grows bright.[3]

Duncan's evocation of a sleeping child and her dreamland adventures provides an abundance of magical images for the young child being read to at bedtime.

Other Children's Books

Duncan has written stories for younger children as well. *Wonder Kid Meets the Evil Lunch Snatcher* (1988) is the story of Brian and Sarah, the new kids in school. The school bully makes a practice of stealing his classmates' lunches, and the newcomers decide to get even. They invent Wonder Kid, a super hero, and rig up an outfit and special effects for Brian, who then proceeds to teach the bully a lesson.

Duncan's earlier books for younger children include *Silly Mother* (1962), *The Littlest One in the Family* (1960), and *Giving Away Suzanne* (1963). These were stories inspired by Duncan's own children.

Another book, this one for slightly older children, reflects Duncan's affection for animals. Entitled *Hotel for Dogs*, it was first published in 1971. Liz, a dog lover, and her family have moved from Albuquerque to a town in New Jersey where they are temporarily living with an older relative allergic to animals. Liz is resentful at being forced to put her beloved Bebe, a dachshund, into a temporary home.

Liz and her older brother Bruce immediately dislike the boy next door, Jerry, because he mistreats his fine Irish setter. When the dog runs away, Liz decides to hide him in a vacant house in the neighborhood, along with a stray who has had puppies. Another stray joins the ménage, along with a friend's set of crossbred puppies, and the dog hotel gets mighty full. The kids become increasingly taxed with taking care of the dogs—getting enough food for them, grooming and exercising them, finding homes for new puppies—and keeping Jerry from finding out that his Irish setter is still in the neighborhood.

The climax comes when a realtor shows the house to Liz's mother (Dad's new job is going to be in the same town) and the hotel for dogs is discovered. All ends happily, of course. Even Jerry is found out by his parents, who finally see him for the little rat he really is.

Non-thriller Books for Young Adults

Duncan found her major niche as a writer early. As an aspiring author in her teen years, she wrote about the things she knew, and she has continued to write about teens throughout her life, even though she has written for other age groups as well. Duncan tried her hand at a number of different kinds of books for young adults before specializing in suspense tales.

Two of these books are historical. One, *Major Andre: Brave Enemy,* is nonfiction, one of a series about famous spies. This was followed by *Peggy* in 1970, a fictionalized biography of Peggy Shippen, wife of General Benedict Arnold. The story focuses on her life as a teenager during the Revolutionary War. Duncan's intention was probably to portray an historical figure as a sympathetic, believable young woman to teen readers of today. Much attention is paid to the flirtations and romances of Peggy and her sisters. In the end, however, Peggy does not come across as a sympathetic person at all, but rather a selfish, frivolous, and shallow young woman.

Debutante Hill

Lois Duncan's first book-length manuscripts were centered on teen characters of the 1950s, when they were written. The first one to be completed was *Love Song for Joyce,* but the first one published was *Debutante Hill,* the winner of Dodd, Mead's Seventeenth Summer Literary Competition. The book was serialized in *Compact* magazine, then a popular periodical for teens. Duncan was inspired to write the book when her young brother Bill told her about the advent of a debutante system in her hometown. Her reaction was:

> What a sad season, I thought, for a girl whose friends were chosen to be "debs," but who herself was excluded from all the dances and parties. How might such a girl be affected by this experience? How would she be changed as a person?
>
> I fashioned the girl after myself, named her Lynn, and placed her in the familiar setting of my own high school years. The town was Sarasota, renamed Rivertown (*Chapters,* 230)

Lynn Chambers is a golden girl who has it all. She lives with her perfect nuclear family (her father is a doctor) in the best part of town, the Hill. Her senior year of high school begins with only one cloud; her boyfriend Paul has departed for college.

Then Mrs. Peterson, mother of awkward Brenda, decides to start a debutante system in town. Twenty girls (including Brenda and primarily residents of the Hill) will be invited to participate in an exclusive social season, culminating in a presentation ball. Lynn is invited, but her father insists that she decline. He is very opposed to the exclusive nature of the deb season, and urges Lynn to be more democratic in her choice of friends.

> "You didn't mean it, did you, Daddy, about not liking the idea of my making a debut? Everybody is going to be doing it."
>
> "Everybody in Rivertown?"
>
> "No, of course not, but all my good friends are—Nancy and Holly and Joan, oh, all the girls on the Hill. It will be just 'the thing' this year."
>
> "It may be 'the thing,'" Dr. Chambers said slowly, "but that doesn't make it right. It's something I don't like to see starting. There is already a disturbing quality growing in this town, a

> separating of the people according to where they live and how
> much money they have, a feeling that doesn't belong in a place of
> this size. It's bad enough when it exists among the adult popula-
> tion, but it's a tragedy to carry it down into the schools. A public
> school should be a mixing place, an opportunity for all the young
> people of the town to get to know each other."[4]

Feeling left out of the things that count, Lynn also finds her old friends distancing themselves from her. A tough kid from school, Dirk Masters, almost dares her to date him, and Lynn accepts. Dirk runs with an "outcast" crowd reminiscent of the 1957 film *Rebel without a Cause* and predating S. E. Hinton's *The Outsiders* (1967). Lynn rather likes Dirk, who obviously has a crush on her, but feels uncomfortable. She avoids accepting another date.

Paul comes home for Christmas vacation, but rather than date Lynn, he gets drafted to be Brenda's escort at all the in parties on "Debutante Hill." Lynn is resentful, and goes out with Dirk the next time he asks.

Dirk gives Lynn a pearl necklace that had belonged to his dead mother. Lynn later regrets having accepted it and tries to give it back. Dirk, however, is angry when Lynn says that she cannot care for him as he cares for her, and he rejects her offer of friendship.

Lynn has become friendly with Dirk's sister, Anne, having wisely listened to her own younger sister's advice that she mix around and get new friends. She finds that there are people worth knowing besides her former close friends on Debutante Hill.

The climax of the deb season is the presentation ball during spring break. It is a charity event to raise money for the hospi-tal—a blatant attempt to quiet Dr. Chambers, who is agitating around town about the evils of the debutante system. Five hun-dred dollars is raised, but the cash is stolen from Brenda's car be-fore it can be delivered. Dirk is accused of the crime based on circumstantial evidence, and he is expelled from school. Brenda tries unsuccessfully to implicate Lynn as party to the theft.

Lynn is sure Dirk is innocent and expresses her views in a letter to Paul. When Paul returns to town, he suggests that Lynn and he get the goods on the real culprit, an older friend of Dirk's. They manage to do this in a somewhat hokey action scene, and all ends happily. Lynn and Paul are reunited and Brenda sees the error of her ways. Dirk is reconciled to the idea that Lynn will never be his. It is also apparent that the first deb season in Rivertown will be the last.

The Joyce Books

Two other books written by Duncan during the late 1950s were based on Duncan's year as a college student at Duke University. Duncan's mother had saved all the letters her daughter had sent while at Duke, and Duncan used them as the basis for the Joyce books. The books' central character is Joyce Reynolds, and the plots center on Joyce's experiences in college away from home—classes, romance, and the social scene.

Love Song for Joyce begins with Joyce's arrival at Denton University for her freshman year. Her parents have encouraged her to go further away to school than the University of Florida, where most of her friends, including steady boyfriend Frank and best friend Margo, are going.

> Oh, it was a nice enough campus on the whole, Joyce thought bitterly, very neat and green and collegy. The boys' campus, a mile or so away, was really lovely, with ivy climbing the walls of the Gothic-style buildings, tall trees and winding paths and well-kept gardens. If you compared it, it was undoubtedly much handsomer than the University of Florida. But the University would have been friendly and familiar and close to home, and she would have known so many of the people there. Practically everyone in the senior class had gone on to the University. It would have been like continuing high school on another level. Here she was completely alone and did not know a soul.[5]

The plot is a typical junior romance of the 1950s. Joyce gets a crush on musically talented Ed, overlooking the fine, steady qualities of premed Jeff until the book's end. There are relationships with the other girls in the dorm, such as Joyce's disappointment with studious Stella as a roommate and her concern for over-weight, reclusive Kathy down the hall.

The most substantial part of the story deals with Joyce's atti-tudes about sororities. She is at first caught up in the hyperbole of pledge week and joins the sorority of her friends Betty and Con-nie. She has doubts about the exclusiveness of such organizations, however, and is concerned about Kathy when she does not get a bid. It is Jeff who makes Joyce see her true feelings:

> "Yes," Joyce admitted, "I have." She looked from her parents to Jeff to Kathy, and suddenly she knew what she was going to do. "I have pledged," she said sturdily, "but I'm with Kathy all the way on this. I think she's absolutely right. Since I've been a pledge I have hardly had time for anything else. I've neglected my studies, I hardly know what my roommate looks like any-more. If I had not been spending all my time at pledge meetings and playing bridge at the sorority house, my term paper would be done by now. Besides, I've seen too many girls, nice girls, hurt terribly by not being included in a sorority. No club should have the power to hurt anybody that much." (*Love Song*, 203)

A Promise for Joyce is the story of Joyce's sophomore year at Denton. Immediately, Joyce has a fight with Jeff—he's spending too much time in medical school and not enough time with her. Joyce becomes poetry editor of Denton's literary magazine, where she meets Bill, a polio victim consigned to a wheelchair. Conflict arises over the aims of the literary magazine—Bill and Joyce want it to have more popular appeal, while the editor, Ginny (Bill's love interest) wants to maintain the high literary quality of the journal.

The romance of this novel centers on Joyce's friend Betty, who is involved with a fast boy who drives a fast car. Joyce's own love life is quiet, with casual dates. Kathy has lost weight and is doing fine in the social scene. Stella still concentrates on her studies, but enjoys a vacation with Joyce's family. There are many clues that in spite of Joyce's immaturity in her treatment of Jeff, she is growing up emotionally.

The climax of the book comes when Joyce and Betty are on a double date and are in a car accident. In the aftermath of shock and fear, Joyce calls Jeff, who valiantly comes to the rescue, and she collapses happily in his arms.

Joyce's story does not continue through the rest of her college career and beyond, like other series books. It is probably just as well, since it might be a bit hard to take Joyce's inevitable marriage to Jeff and a subsequent version of television's *The Donna Reed Show*.

The Middle Sister

Duncan wrote one other book for young adults in the 1950s. A representative junior novel of the time, *The Middle Sister* was published in 1960 and tells about a nice teenager and her year as a high school junior.

Ruth Porter is the middle sister, sandwiched between her siblings Janet and Amy. Janet is away at college, but her sparkling personality still overshadows Ruth, who tries to emulate the older girl. Janet is talented at dramatics, and shy, tall Ruth also tries to excel in theater. By a fluke, she lands a leading character role in the local community theater production, where she meets the new young director, Kent Darrow.

Ruth and Kent become friends, and Ruth invites him to her family's thanksgiving dinner. Janet is home from college, and there is an immediate, obvious attraction between Janet and Kent. Ruth is disappointed and hurt, but she continues the school year on an even emotional keel.

The youngest Porter girl, Amy, is an intense fifteen-year-old. She writes poetry and already has a steady boyfriend, David Richmond. When David suddenly cools his relationship with Amy, the confused girl asks her sister Ruth to find out from David's older brother Jerry what's wrong. Ruth discovers that David, due in part to pressure from his parents, has decided his relationship with Amy is too serious and wants to date other girls. As Ruth and Jerry are talking in the Richmond's driveway, an accident occurs at the corner. Ruth and Jerry run to a smashed car where they discover an injured woman inside. Jerry is shaken, but Ruth crawls into the car and temporarily stops the bleeding. When the ambulance arrives, the woman's life is saved, due to Ruth's quick thinking.

Ruth and Jerry had always been friends, but now Jerry seems to have more than a casual interest in Ruth. He asks her to the Christmas formal at school, and Ruth accepts. She is getting over her crush on Kent and is pleased with the help she gets in picking out a smashing formal dress from Janet's tall, glamorous friend who is visiting for the holidays.

As Ruth's year progresses, she sees her sister Janet's feelings for Kent becoming more serious, and her other sister Amy's poetry writing becoming good enough to be submitted to a contest. Ruth's feelings for Jerry deepen, but she remains uncertain of her own plans for after high school.

Family disaster occurs when Ruth's mother falls and requires bedrest. Ruth volunteers to be her mother's "nurse," and finds her nurturing, caring instincts blossoming. By the end of the book it is clear that Ruth is destined to be a nurse.

Two Books about New Mexico

After her move to New Mexico following her divorce, Duncan was obviously inspired by her new surroundings. At least two books, one for teens and one for adults, were the result. The earlier one, *Season of the Two-Heart* (1964), tells about the life of a Native American teenager.

Natachu (Martha) Weekoty is a Pueblo girl living in New Mexico. Missionaries on her reservation make arrangements for Martha to spend her year of high school senior in Albuquerque, so she can attend a good school and have a chance to earn a scholarship for college. Martha is placed as a mother's helper with the Boynton family in Albuquerque, where her chief job is to look after two young boys, Dan and Teddy. Dan is wary of people in general, but Teddy is an exuberant, affectionate child, obviously his mother's favorite. Martha does not anticipate problems with the boys, but she is a bit hurt by their older sister's snubbing of Martha because she is a Native American.

Martha gradually makes friends and is given the opportunity to sing in the school chorus, where she becomes increasingly attached to Alan Wallace. She is troubled by cultural pulls, for she has always intended to return home to the reservation and marry a dashing young man there. Her mother and grandmother had both warned her of becoming a "two-heart," neither white nor Indian, someone with no true identity.

As with most young adult novels of the early 1960s, things resolve themselves fairly well by the end of the story. Martha is given the opportunity to develop her beautiful singing voice, and even becomes friends with snotty Laurie Boynton. She helps Mrs. Boynton come to the realization that she needs to show more love for Dan. She also demonstrates enough good sense to tell Alan that they are too young to get married—unlike Lois Duncan herself, who married at nineteen. Martha even has a book of her translations of her people's songs published. She feels that her true future lies back at the pueblo as a teacher, where she can help her people to a better life.

When the Bough Breaks, (1973) is a woman's book, written for an adult audience, and told in first-person narrative by Kate Michener, divorced mother of three living in Albuquerque. Her oldest child is Diane, a teenager with a boyfriend, Paul. Susan and Christopher are younger kids. Kate works as a free-lance advertising copywriter, and is involved with a young commercial artist at the agency, Dan McCown.

Kate suspects she is pregnant and goes to a doctor for confirmation. Her cautious inquiries reveal that the doctor is unwilling to perform a controversial operation. She tells Dan, who offers to arrange an abortion for her. They go across the border to Mexico, where a retired American doctor has agreed to perform the operation under sterile conditions. Just as the doctor is ready to start, Kate realizes that she cannot have the abortion; she will keep the baby.

Diane is anxious to see her father, now remarried and living in Florida. When the family vacations in Florida, the children visit with their father, and Kate stays with her parents. Kate's parents discover she is pregnant, and Kate lets them think she and Dan plan to get married. Dan does write to Kate offering to marry her, but Kate is oddly reluctant. Dan has a chance at a job at a big agency in New York. Being ambitious, he pursues it.

Kate and the children return to Albuquerque. Dan has said he'll be interviewing in New York, but Kate finds out from Pete, the head of the ad agency, that Dan has already accepted the New York job. People react conservatively to Kate's pregnancy. She had agreed to be an assistant Girl Scout leader for Susan, but at the last minute she is told that they don't need her. Diane behaves badly and becomes openly rebellious. Dan returns to Albuquerque to tie up loose ends and again offers marriage. He is relieved when Kate refuses.

Just before the baby is due, Diane breaks up with Paul, has a ripsnorting fight with Kate, who slaps her, and flees to be with her father in Florida. Kate explains the situation to her ex-husband's new wife, who assures her Diane will be welcome. Diane's father, however, tells her that she cannot stay and ships her back to New Mexico, where the seemingly contrite girl asks her mother's forgiveness.

The evening of Diane's return, Kate's baby is born. In the closing pages of the novel, Kate's labor produces a baby boy. Kate names the child John after her own beloved father.

It is apparent in this book that Duncan uses the character of Kate to describe her own—Duncan's—sense of place and feelings about nature. Like Duncan, Kate grew up in Florida and relocated to Albuquerque after her divorce. The following passage may well be descriptive of Duncan's own feelings about these locales: "As in the West I find my strength in the mountains, here it is by the water. I spend long hours walking along the shoreline, feeling the waves lap my toes, stooping now and then to pick up a shell to put aside for Chris on his return" (*When*, 78).

Most of the books written by Duncan during the 1950s and early 1960s are now out of print. They were not bad books, but they were reflective of the time in which they were written. Society has changed, and the attitudes and actions of the characters are simply not typical of people in today's world. Duncan herself has referred to her first book, *Debutante Hill,* as "sweet and sticky and pap, but in the 1950s that's the kind of book teenagers read."[6] Today's teenagers would find Duncan's early romance novels as foreign to them as novels of the ancient world.

3. The Early Thrillers

Lois Duncan could view herself as a successful writer by 1960, while she was still in her twenties. She had written and published many articles, stories, and poems, as well as three books. She had obviously followed MacKinley Kantor's advice about basing her works on her own experiences and what she knew firsthand. She had published pieces about adolescence while still a teen herself. She had written about being a college student, wife, and young mother, as she moved through these experiences. Her writing skills were becoming sharper, and her lean, direct prose style was adaptable to many different kinds of writing.

Duncan's work up to this time had included poetry, anecdotal articles, one prize-winning young adult novel, two romances, and a number of magazine stories. She had moved into writing full-length books easily, already proficient in plot and character development. Her versatility is evident in the ease with which she moved from one type of project to the next.

Duncan enjoys reading mysteries and thrillers, so it is not surprising that she decided to try her hand at writing them, beginning in the 1960s. Her early attempts show some of the characteristics that would make her young adult thrillers so popular with teenage readers: realistic characters, page-turning action, careful plotting, and focus on the theme of personal integrity.

An early example of Duncan's suspense stories for teens can be found in a story published in *Seventeen* magazine in April and May 1961. Entitled "Face in the Window," the two-part serial uses familiar Duncan themes: a child in peril, a brave teenage hero, a romance subplot, and effective use of Florida as a setting.

Duncan's first book-length thriller was *Game of Danger* (1962). This book is not particularly appealing to today's readers, primarily because of its Cold War setting, but it is still an exciting story for those not put off by the anti-Communist message.

Game of Danger

Blond Anne McQuarter is the new kid in high school. Her father is a teacher at the school as well, and since students are often wary of "teachers' kids," she is grateful for the friendship of some popular seniors. She is a bit uneasy that there is so much emphasis on extracurricular activities at the cost of academics in her new school, but only the editor of the high school paper, David, seems to share that opinion.

At the start of the book, Anne and her fourteen-year-old brother, Rob, are awakened by their German-born mother. They are given hurried, whispered instructions along with an envelope to keep safe. They are to slip out of the house at once and go by bus to their mother's friend in Maine. They are extremely puzzled, but Rob refers to it all as a game of danger. When they arrive at the address of their mother's friend, however, they discover she no longer resides there. Knowing they must be careful, they check into a hotel, where Anne lets Rob cut her beautiful long hair, which might be a giveaway to anyone on the lookout for them.

They read in the newspaper that their father has disappeared and is accused of being a Communist agent. Unable to trust anyone, they find that their mother doesn't want them to telephone her. They contact their mother's friend at her new address, but she has no information and urges them to return home. As they make ready to leave, Anne discovers to her horror that the envelope she had hidden in the refrigerator freezer has gotten wet and the contents are ruined.

Arriving back home, Anne and Rob learn from an FBI agent that their father has been working for the FBI all along, but that Communists had threatened their mother's relatives still in East Germany. The Communists have kidnapped Mr. McQuarter. Anne has a plan to get him back; she and Rob will return to school and serve as bait, since the Communists are still after the contents of the envelope—a handwritten copy of a secret U.S. official document.

The plan works after some delays and suspense. Anne and Rob discover most of their friends believe that their father is a Communist and snub them, except for David. In the end, Mr. McQuarter is recovered, and it is revealed that the ringleader of the local Communist group is none other than the president of the school board.

Although the paranoic days of the McCarthy era had ended by the time Duncan published *Game of Danger,* Communism was still viewed as a subversive doctrine in this country, which was yet to experience the Cuban missile crisis and other East-West power struggles. Even knowing the historical context, however, it is still a bit hard to swallow some of the preaching, "'Just imagine,' exclaimed Mother, 'if there was one Communist agent on every school board in the country! What would become of this rising generation? What would we do ten years from now for engineers and doctors and scientists and statesmen?' She turned to Dad in horror, 'And to think, I was so grateful to Marge Gilmore for finding this house for us to rent, right next door to their own! It seemed like such a nice, friendly thing for her to do.'"[1]

Reviews of this early Duncan thriller were brief, yet the story was praised as having a "different theme for teen-age stories, not without romantic subplot,"[2] and for being "an exciting story, well told and fast-paced, with good characterizations."[3] Already Duncan's characteristic writing style was developed enough to be noticed by critics.

Duncan uses the example of this book to describe her frustration, early in her writing career, with publishers who were conservative and cautious.

> *Game of Danger* was the story of a girl and her brother . . . who were engaged in a wild chase through New England in an effort to keep secret documents out of the hands of the "bad guys." Midway through the book, too exhausted to flee further, they stopped at an inn, rented a room, and slept for a couple of hours.
> This chapter came back with exclamation marks in the margin.
> "You have two people of opposite sexes sharing a room and they're not married!"
> "But they're brother and sister," I protested. "They're fully clothed, and they're lying on twin beds."
> "That makes no difference," my editor said. "Librarians would never touch a book that included such a suggestive scene. You will have to have them rent separate rooms."
> Since my characters had almost no money, I could not image their doing such a thing. Still, I didn't want to offend the nation's librarians. We finally reached a compromise with an L-shaped alcove in which the boy could nap out of sight of his sister. (SAA:AS, 71)

Point of Violence

Duncan's next thriller was not written for teens. *Point of Violence* is an adult mystery, a Doubleday Crime Club Selection published in 1966. The book takes place in Florida, and features a widowed mother, and the reader can well image the now divorced Duncan having many of the same thoughts.

Julia Culler's husband, Mark, had been killed two years before in a waterskiing accident. Julia is still shocked by his loss, and she clings to the remote house on a Florida Gulf key they had built together. Their small children, Brud (Mark Junior) and Cam have adapted, but Julia still mourns Mark, cherishing memories of their short time together. Now twenty-seven, Julia earns her living as a children's book illustrator—Mark had been a successful young novelist. Julia's widowed mother, Kate, is recently remarried to Wesley, and Julia's sister, Andi, and her lawyer husband, Bill, all live in nearby Palmelo. Julia has maintained good relations with an old friend, Lucy Braile, although she cannot forgive Roger Braile, her brother and Julia's possessive high school beau, for his part in the accident that had killed Mark.

It is obvious to Julia that someone is trying to harm her children. Accidents keep happening. Finally, her house is set on fire, and Brud is burned, placing him in the hospital. Julia becomes reacquainted with Ted Grenville, whom she had dated casually in high school, now a doctor. Andi and Bill's marriage seems a bit strained; perhaps their consuming desire for children is a problem. Lucy, a plain girl, is deliriously excited over a new boyfriend she has met in Miami.

Julia distrusts Roger intensely. She goes to his home after Brud is burned and finds Roger murdered. It seems that everyone is a candidate for the crime: Julia to protect her children; Kate (and Wesley) because Wesley's daughter from an earlier marriage was killed in a car accident caused by drunken Roger while he was still in law school; and Andi because she had been seduced and impregnated by Roger while still in high school and the consequent abortion had sterilized her. Lucy doesn't seem terribly rational either, especially after she finds out her new boyfriend is married.

In the end, it turns out that Andi is the culprit, and that she is somewhat unbalanced. She kills herself. Julia is stunned, but realizes that she is ready for life without Mark, and possibly Ted (or even now-widowed Bill) may be romantic interests for her.

As a book club selection, *Point of Violence* sold fairly well, but the critical reception of the book was mixed at best. *Best Sellers* described the story as "nicely plotted and something of a change, too."[4] *Kirkus*, however, labeled it "a distraught distraction, only for the girls."[5] The mystery review column for the *New York Times Book Review* called it "reasonably readable if you like highly emotional idiot heroines in Florida settings, and don't mind overdrawn and underdrawn characters and fairly messy plotting."[6] Alice Cromie in *Books Today* called the book promotion "sneaky," since the publisher billed it as a suspense title, rather than a "Damsel in Distress."[7]

Ransom

Published in 1966, Duncan's next suspense book for young adults, *Ransom* (also entitled *Five Were Missing*), met with a ready audience of teenage readers. Her usual publisher, however, did not want to handle the thriller since it was a departure from her earlier books. Having been challenged by Robin, her oldest daughter, to write an exciting book for readers her age, Duncan wrote a novel that many young adults found exciting. Duncan considers this book an important one because it made her known to librarians. This would be the start of Duncan's recognition as a "name-brand author," whose books librarians are asked for by name: "Do you have any Lois Duncans I haven't read?"

Ransom has an exciting plot, but it is also notable for its characters. This aspect of the novel is reminiscent of the popular John Hughes's film *The Breakfast Club,* in which five disparate adolescents discover a great deal about themselves and each other on a day of detention. *Ransom,* written long before the 1985 film, even has the same number of young people involved, three boys and two girls. The characters are not as patly defined as in *The Breakfast Club:* the Princess, the Basketcase, the Brain, the Jock, and the Criminal. Yet each of the *Ransom* characters is clearly delineated, and their growing awareness of each other is an important part of the book.

The plot of *Ransom* revolves around the kidnapping of five high schoolers. Duncan introduces us to each character, explaining why they are on the bus that day, and how they interact with the others. Since they live in an upscale part of town—the last bus stop—the kidnappers assume they will have a controllable number of victims worth high ransoms.

The five teens are Glenn and Bruce Kirtland, Marianne Paget, Jesse French, and Dexter Barton. Glenn Kirtland is a handsome, unfeeling, selfish egocentric. His young brother, Bruce, is shy, overshadowed by his brother, whom he worships. Marianne is Glenn's girlfriend, bitter about her mother's remarriage and yearning for her dashing father's attentions. Jesse is a cosmopolitan army brat, but diffident and awkward around her peers. Dexter, slightly crippled from polio, has been recently orphaned and is now living with a playboy-type bachelor uncle who lets Dexter take care of himself.

"They were nice people, all of them bright, normal, above-average teen-agers from good backgrounds. They brushed their teeth and said their prayers and made good grades in high school and they would go to college and marry and enter various professions. Dreadful things did not happen to people like this."[8] Duncan's description of teenage attitudes of invincibility is illustrative of the views of the five protagonists in the early pages of the story.

There are three villains. The kidnappers are handsome Buck and plain Rita, along with Juan who kills the regular bus driver so that Buck can take his place. After the five teens are driven past their turnoff, they are told that they are being held for ransom and are taken to a deserted cabin in the mountains. It is during their hours of captivity in the cabin that the teens learn about themselves and one another, producing ever-changing group dynamics.

Glenn assumes that he is the leader of the beleaguered group. Yet his comments and ideas for escape reveal his view of himself as a hero, always in the center, and uncaring of others. Bruce comes to realize his brother's basic coldness. Bitter Dexter lashes out at Glenn, and Glenn later broods on the other boy's words: "That tirade, for instance, about feeling things. That was a crazy subject for a person to get steamed up about. He personally couldn't care less about the way Dexter felt about things. Why couldn't everybody just take the world as it came and stop getting emotional about it? Yet there was one thing the boy had said which bothered him. That part about not loving. *I bet you've never really loved anybody in your whole life!*" (*Ransom*, 75). Even Marianne sees Glenn's basic cynicism. Dexter and Jesse were the first to be disillusioned, but Dexter's sullen personality and Jesse's quietness hid that from the others.

When the kidnappers contact the families of the teens, there is the expected shock and terror. Yet even the Kirtlands' reaction includes clues about Glenn's personality, such as this comment from his mother: "'I never thought you noticed. He is so handsome, so strong, so wonderful in so many ways. Yet sometimes when I'm close to him, when I give him a hug or kiss him, I look into his eyes—and there's nothing in them. I mean, he has beautiful eyes, but they're empty.' She shuddered. 'I'm being silly. Tell me I'm being silly, Steve, that I'm all upset and worked up'" (*Ransom*, 81).

Jesse and Dexter find themselves drawn to each other, even as Marianne's feelings for Glenn are cooling. But all of this sexual underplay is secondary to the real problem the teens face, the need to escape, or at least to prevent themselves from getting killed.

In the end all agree to a plan to escape while Rita and Buck are sleeping. Dexter will hotwire the station wagon, and with luck they will make their getaway safely. Their plan does not go smoothly, however, and Dexter is shot in the shoulder. Glenn and Bruce make an escape on foot hoping to get through in time to save the others. Buck pursues them, but he crashes the car on a curve and is killed. Glenn and Bruce are separated, and Glenn proceeds down the mountain with dreams of a triumphant return in his head. En route he is intercepted by Juan and Marianne's stepfather, supposedly coming with the ransom money.

But there is no ransom money. The Kirtlands were able to put enough together and also volunteered to help Jesse's mother who is unable to reach her husband. Marianne's father had refused to take calls from his ex-wife, and her money had not been contributed. The kidnappers had never reached Dexter's uncle, away for the weekend.

Marianne's stepfather is desperately bluffing. He has a gun in lieu of the money and is going to try to rescue the victims by himself. He manages to do this with the help of the kids in an action-packed finale. In the end, all the teens are rescued, and they all realize important things about themselves and others.

Glenn is probably the least affected, although he has been forced to think critically about himself and his values. Nevertheless, he probably will not change his behavior or attitudes.

Bruce realizes that he has stopped worshipping his older brother. He is his own person and sees Glenn more clearly than ever before.

Marianne understands at last that her father doesn't care about her, and her despised new stepfather obviously has much more love for her than her father ever did.

Dexter loses some of his bitterness and is proud of his heroic behavior under stress. He is also happy about his romantic involvement with Jesse.

Jesse, the most reflective of the characters, doesn't change significantly, although she is pleased by her improved social skills with those her own age.

By switching viewpoints among the five main characters, Duncan provides us with personal glimpses of very different people. Although this is a good device for helping the reader come in contact with various personalities, it is also a technique which results in no one teen being the dominant character. It would probably not have been easy to make Glenn the major protagonist since he is so unsympathic, but in many ways Marianne is the one who comes across as the most sharply delineated character in the group, and the subplot regarding her relationship with her stepfather is the most interesting.

Duncan's technique of shifting the viewpoint does not work as well in *Ransom* as it does in later books such as *Daughters of Eve*. Distributing the point of view among the many different personalities of the characters results in a more splintered effect in building tension. It is difficult for an author to present well-rounded characters, use their different viewpoints, and still provide a plot that builds steadily toward a climax. Duncan is able to do this more successfully in later books. The lack of complete success here may be partly due to the fact that at this point in her writing career she was better able to depict female characters as three-dimensional, while the male characters—with the exception of Glenn—are flatter, more stereotypical.

One advantage of using many different characters in a book is that more readers will find characters who appeal to them. One reader wrote to Duncan: "I just read *Ransom*. I feel like I am in love with Dexter. The way Jesse was firm with him and made him trust her was so wonderful. I was so happy when she kissed him!"[9]

The plot of *Ransom* is direct, unlike Robert Cormier's *After the First Death,* another young adult novel dealing with a school bus kidnapping. Patty Campbell calls the plot of the latter "a fairly complex structure with built-in puzzles and trapdoors."[10] *Ransom,* however, presents a straightforward situation evocative of today's newspaper headlines in which the victims must do their best to circumvent a terrifying, almost surreal, situation.

In the *New York Times Book Review* Dorothy Broderick described the character of Glenn as "thoroughly amoral, egocentric . . . a character unique in children's books, though not in life." She went on to conclude, "It is this consistency of Glenn's personality that sets the book apart and makes it something more than another good mystery."[11]

Duncan makes no references to Glenn being based on a real person, as Mark was in *Killing Mr. Griffin.* Yet the character is a believable one, and one that most people admit to having known at some time in their lives. There are teenagers like Glenn, just as there are adults like him. Glenn is more than the "normal" teen who is generally preoccupied with the self; Glenn is the kind of person who may go through life with no feelings for others. Duncan's message might well be that teens need to recognize people like this, for those who are unfeeling can be extremely hurtful to others in their thoughtlessness and selfishness.

Ransom was a runner-up for the Edgar Allan Poe Award in the junior novel category. Duncan always seems to be an "also ran" for this prestigious award from the Mystery Writers of America, although her fans, no doubt, have faith that someday she will add this accomplishment to the other awards she has received throughout the years. The quality of *Ransom* was part of the justification for the 1992 Margaret A. Edwards Award. The announcement comments that "the five kidnapped young adults in 'Ransom,' along with Tracy Lord from 'The Twisted Window,' not only find inner strengths to escape from someone who has taken over their lives, but they also discover a sense of community in working with and helping others" (ALA Press Release, 1).

They Never Came Home

During the 1960s, Duncan continued to write a variety of works, but in 1969 another young adult thriller, *They Never Came Home*, was published. By the late 1960s the counterculture had glamorized the use of drugs for many young people, and this book comments on that fact. Duncan has always kept track of societal shifts. She comments: "One major change [in young adult novels] is the sophisticated subject matter that is now deemed appropriate for teenagers. The first book [*Debutante Hill*] I wrote was returned for revision, because in it I had a 19-year-old drink a beer. Today, there are books for young people on every subject imaginable, from alcoholism to premarital sex to mental illness" (DD Pamphlet, 3).

The tale of a really bad kid, *They Never Came Home* is a dark story in many ways. Larry, a high school student, takes his sister's boyfriend, decent Don Cotwell, who is suffering from amnesia after a fall in the Mogollon Mountains of New Mexico, on a weekend camping trip. Larry and Don never return from this trip, and after a prolonged search, they are presumed dead. Larry's sister, Joan Drayfus, is therefore hit with a double blow, but proves to be the emotional mainstay of her family. Her father copes, but her mother succumbs to a nervous breakdown and is placed in a sanitarium [*sic*].

Joan (a tall, not terribly pretty girl) tries to get on with her life, but is approached by John Brown, a mysterious man who tells her Larry had been smuggling jewelry designs across the Mexican border for him and has absconded with over $2,000 of Brown's money. Joan finds no money in Larry's room, and his bank account has been emptied. Joan also finds that some of Larry's favorite clothes are missing.

In the meantime, Larry (calling himself Lance) has taken Don (now called Dave) to California, where he convinces Don that they are orphaned brothers. Don gets a job to support them (as a mature-looking high school senior, he is apparently able to do this even without ID), and Larry becomes a beach bum. Don is attracted to a girl, Peggy, who reminds him of Joan, the old girlfriend trapped below his present consciousness level.

Back in Las Cruces, Joan tells Brown she will try to earn the money Larry owes. He suggests that she take on Larry's job of jewelry-running across the Mexican border. Joan agrees, but Don's younger brother, Frank, is suspicious and insists on going along. Joan and Frank have become good friends, but there is no romance between them. Neither Joan nor Frank see anything special about the jewelry designs they are smuggling for Brown. On one trip their car gets a flat tire, and Frank finds marijuana hidden in the hub cap. It is now plain that drugs are the real items being smuggled from Mexico by John Brown. Joan reluctantly faces up to the truth of rumors that Larry had been a high school drug pusher, but doesn't tell her parents. Frank and Joan tell the police and help them get the evidence to arrest Brown.

In California, Don's memory is returning in flashes, and he forces Larry to tell him the full story. Don is recognized by a friend of Joan's now at UCLA. Joan goes to California, and in a dramatic climax Larry tries to push Don off their apartment balcony, but instead falls to his own death. Not telling Joan this, Don just says they are going home.

One of Duncan's strongest antidrug polemics is uttered by one of the teen characters:

> Maybe the kids at the party had truly believed that smoking marijuana "just once" would be a harmless fling. Frank had heard enough and read enough to know better. There was never anything "one time" about dope, no matter what its form. At the next party it would have been there again, except then there would have been a charge for it. Then, before long, it would not be confined to parties. Kids would be buying it privately, smoking it at home in their bedrooms, in school rest rooms, on dates in parked cars. It would become "old stuff," no longer thrilling or

different. And then there would be a *new* party, at which stronger drugs would be introduced.[12]

This message is a little easier to accept from a teen. Another commentary, this time delivered by an adult, the villainous Brown, involves another subject, that of gender roles: "I'm glad the Drayfus girl isn't with you tonight," Mr. Brown began. "Girls are fine in their place, but, as I mentioned before, their place isn't in the world of business. It takes a man, with a man's logic, to understand what a real business opportunity is. Larry Drayfus was that kind of young man. He had a sharp business sense, a lot of ambition.' He paused. 'How about you, Frank? Are you ambitious?'" (*They*, 166).

Although criticized by some reviewers for its contrived plot, *They Never Came Home* was praised by critic Richard F. Shephard as "a well-paced action story, with a full quota of heroes and villains, and a series of narrative hooks guaranteed to hold any reader."[13] This reviewer makes a good point, for there is a suitable villain and hero/heroine for the two main settings of the book, New Mexico and California. Larry is as self-centered and uncaring as Glenn Kirtland in *Ransom,* and drug dealer Brown is obviously unscrupulous. Don/Dave is a clean-cut youth, and the reader readily sympathizes with and relates to him and Joan. In fact, much of the action is centered on the male characters, and one feels almost cheated that more time isn't spent with Joan, a mature, sensible, and thoroughly likeable young woman.

Shephard also commends Duncan's writing:

> [She] writes well and simply on mature situations. She gives her readers comprehensible, yet not oversensational descriptions of a mother's nervous breakdown; of a plain girl discovering beauty in herself; of a younger brother learning not to live in the reflected glory of an older one; of a mentally deranged boy who has cut himself off from the love his family wanted to give him. "They Never Came Home" is a well-paced action story, with a full quota of heroes and villains and a series of narrative hooks guaranteed to hold any reader. (Shephard, 42)

Duncan's thrillers demonstrate her interest in dual personalities, disguises, and role playing. She is able to present a variety of situations and motivations in which different personas are used. In *Game of Danger,* Anne and Rob use disguises simply to protect themselves in a perilous situation. In *Ransom,* Glenn Kirtland has been playing a role his whole life, covering his cold heart with a veneer of sensitivity. In *They Never Came Back,* there is the contrast of dual personalities. One, Larry, is performing in a knowing and calculating way, while the other, Don, has been victimized by Larry into developing a whole new personality as a result of his temporary amnesia. These are plot twists that Duncan has used effectively in her writing, and that teenage readers find appealing, for in addition to loving fast-paced action stories, teens are very interested in personalities, their own and those of their friends.

Duncan's skill at writing thrillers was obviously becoming more practiced with *They Never Came Back.* Before her next young adult thriller, *I Know What You Did Last Summer,* was to be published in 1975, however, Duncan was to explore a new suspense element in her books, that of psychic and supernatural phenomena.

4. The Occult and Psychic Novels

The supernatural, a level of experience that cannot be explained by present human knowledge, is an intriguing subject for many writers, including those who write teen fiction. There's nothing like spooky houses, ghosts, and eerie beings to create a mood of fascination that keeps the reader turning pages. Occult themes have long enthralled storytellers and their listeners.

During the twentieth century some scientists have attempted to apply scientific principles to supernatural manifestations. These scientists, often called parapsychologists, have identified certain supernatural areas for investigation, particularly those dealing with psychic occurrences, and have conducted experiments with out-of-body experiences, life after death, clairvoyance, and other phenomena.

A number of Lois Duncan's young adult thrillers deal with occult and psychic themes. Often, stories featuring supernatural events are considered horror books, a genre that has been very popular with teen readers since the 1970s. Duncan's occult books typically center on young women with unusual problems caused or influenced by unnatural events. These novels are among the most popular Duncan has written for teens.

Duncan's occult themes include both psychic and supernatural elements. Psychic phenomena, or, as they are sometimes called,

ESP (for extra-sensory perception), may not be supernatural at all, and scientists continue to study them. Some day they may not be considered occult, or hidden, secrets, but explainable facts, proven by accepted scientific methods. At present, ESP is a controversial though popular subject.

According to J. B. Rhine, one of the early ESP researchers at Duke University:

> On the reception end of the E.S.P. phenomenon there has been the vague inference of some hidden sense . . . a "sixth sense." . . . The usage is not clear as to whether any reception whatever would be regarded as sensory, or whether the selective interception of a special energy pattern by a specialized and localized organ would be meant. No clarity has yet been achieved on this important end of the function of E.S.P. . . .
>
> One may say the evidence for general E.S.P. is good but the theories are bad; and our knowledge of the phenomena needs refinement through variation and improvement of conditions. We need tests for pure telepathy and more of them for pure clairvoyance, made under conditions that enable easy evaluation of significance, provide safe exclusion of other modes of cognition, and introduce variation enough to suggest the relation of E.S.P. to other processes and lead to its natural explanation.[1]

Duncan explains her adoption of psychic themes:

> It was while I was pregnant with Kait that I wrote *A Gift of Magic,* a book about a twelve-year-old girl with extra-sensory perception. This was a major milestone in my career, because it was the first of my books to involve psychic phenomena, a subject teenage readers embraced with delight. That book was so successful, I followed it with others. It wasn't that I believed in the subjects I was writing about—telepathy, precognition, astral projection—but they provided good story material for exciting novels, and a little dose of fantasy never hurt anybody. (*Who,* 55–56)

Years later, after the murder of her daughter, Duncan explored psychic phenomena as part of her own grieving process and today is not the skeptic she once was. In *Who Killed My Daughter?* Duncan reports talking with the director of the Psychical Research Foundation, Dr. William Roll, who told her: "Our psychic relationships are very normal and natural. The only thing that makes them supernormal is that they don't fit with the most plebeian concept of reality. But if you accept the concept that your mind is connected to others—that all of us are placed on this earth to relate to each other—then, 'psychic phenomena' no longer seems phenomenal. We then see these things, not as spooky and supernatural, but simply as manifestations of the way we are" (*Who*, 208).

A Gift of Magic

A book for younger readers of middle school age, *A Gift of Magic* was published in 1971. Nancy, the protagonist, is twelve and has the gift of magic, or ESP. She lives with her family, except for her newly divorced father, in Florida, where the family is trying to adjust to a new life. Nancy's older sister, Kirby, is interested in dance, and their young brother, Brendon—modeled on Duncan's son, Brett—has made a new friend. Nancy is not adjusting to the new life very well. She misses her father and resents her mother's new boyfriend, an old friend from the past.

Bad things start to happen. Kirby falls and hurts her leg badly. Nancy believes that she has caused Kirby's accident by willing her not to go away to a special ballet school. Nancy is devastated by the news that her father has remarried. Brendon and his buddy have built their own boat, and the launching of it ends in disaster, with the tide fast advancing on a sandbar. Nancy's gift of magic helps her rescue Brendon with the aid of her mother's boyfriend. Nancy gains understanding as a result of these events. As explained in a teacher's guide to mystery/ horror novels, "She lets down her barrier and begins to feel better about herself and her own special gift."[2] She learns that she has judged people too quickly, particularly her mother's friend, Tom Duncan.

In the end, events turn about, with everyone more or less adjusting to their lives and conditions. The book concludes with a sly, if not reality-based, note: "After Thomas Duncan and Elizabeth Garrett were married, they had one more child, a daughter. Her name was Lois, and she was born with the gift of storytelling.[3]

Down a Dark Hall

In the early 1970s supernatural themes were popular with the reading public, especially teenagers. Occult adventures were sought after, and Duncan obligingly wrote a young adult gothic novel entitled *Down a Dark Hall*. Here the subject is loss of personal identity and possession. Adolescent readers can readily relate to the horrors of such a theme. To a teenager, who is experiencing the trials and tribulations of developing a personal identity, the idea that it might be possible to loose that identity to another power is rather terrifying.

The story centers on Kit Gordy—modeled after Duncan's daughter Robin—who is an incoming student at Blackwood, a new school in upstate New York for select young women. It is so select, in fact, that Kit is inexplicably chosen for admission over her good friend Tracey, who is smarter than she. Blackwood is a huge, brooding old mansion owned by Madame Duret. There are only two other teachers besides Madame—her handsome son, Jules, and old Professor Farley. A few servants from the nearby village have been firmly instructed to keep to their place and not gossip with the young ladies. There are only four students enrolled in the school: Kit, Sandy, Lynda, and Ruth.

Kit is sure from the moment she first sees Blackwood that it is a place of evil, but she is stuck there, for her mother and new stepfather are off honeymooning in Europe. The other girls are also disturbed by their surroundings, but not unduly so, and all are enchanted with their palatial, old-fashioned bedrooms.

The school has been designed to encourage creativity and help the students develop their special talents, and so the four young women throw themselves into their lessons. Lynda becomes obsessed with painting, Ruth becomes enamored of higher mathe-

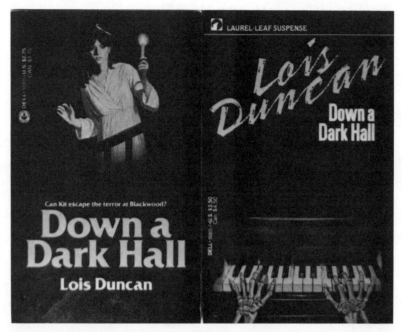

Down a Dark Hall has been published in paperback format a number of times. Two early editions published by Signet depict gothic-style covers with a frail female figure poised fearfully in ominous, dark background. The cover of 1983 (Dell) continues this idea by showing Kit (left) holding a candle and looking uncertainly into darkness. The last cover (Dell, 1990) has eliminated the human figure altogether, along with jacket blurbs. Here, only skeleton hands play a piano keyboard, an obvious marketing ploy to appeal to readers of horror. *Credit: Cam Chasteen*

matics, Sandy discovers an ability to write poetry in French, and Kit finds she is a musical genius.

But these flowering abilities are not normal. The young women react differently to their newfound talents. Lynda paints like one possessed, for she is indeed under the control of the spirit of a dead Hudson River School artist. She turns out beautiful landscape after beautiful landscape with no time spent on anything else, even eating and sleeping. Ruth is excited by her newfound mathematical reasoning, but Kit and Sandy are frightened by the change that has come over them and want to escape from the terrible mansion. Sandy has visions of a woman, and Kit knows she is not herself as she sits at the piano playing skillfully and passionately for hours at a time.

Kit and Sandy are distrustful of their teachers, but Jules seems to be sympathetic to their plight. As it turns out, Madame Duret is an experimental spiritualist who is using the young women as hosts for dead geniuses who continue to create through their bodies. But Madame Duret has not perfected her techniques for this special kind of channeling, and her former experiments of this sort had led to insanity in the hosts.

In a confrontation between Madame Duret and Kit, the older woman justifies her actions, and Kit reacts with vehemence:

> "Privileged!" Kit exploded. "By having my mind used as a receiving unit?" She turned accusingly to Professor Farley. "And, you—you're in on this also?"
>
> "Of course," the professor said. His kindly old face held no trace of guilt. . . .
>
> "I think," Kit said, "that it's the most terrible thing I've ever heard of."
>
> "What's so terrible about it?" Jules asked her. "You ought to be proud."
>
> "Proud of what? That I'm being used, like a tool of some kind?" Kit exclaimed incredulously. The voices from the dream came back to her, and she shuddered uncontrollably. "'She must play for me!' 'I want her tonight!' 'I haven't used her yet!' It's the way you talk about an object, not a person!"[4]

In a fiery climax, Blackwood burns, and Kit almost dies trying to save Lynda. In the end, Madame Duret is thwarted in her plans, and Tracey's parents arrive at just the right moment to fetch Kit back to her old, ordinary existence.

Duncan reports that in her first version of the book all the creative dead geniuses were men. The original manuscript was returned by the publisher, and only after Duncan changed one of the brilliant spirits to a woman was the book accepted for publication. It was explained to her that librarians would not like a book where all the creativity was held by male characters, with the females being used as passive hosts.

Reviewers tended to focus on the gothic qualities of this book. Certainly, the necessary gothic details were included, such as a gloomy old mansion, a mysterious and handsome young man, and nubile young women threatened by supernatural elements. Mystery critic Gloria Levitas saw something more in the book, which she said was "suitably equipped with [a] bright, attractive heroine, a brooding mansion and [a] brooding young man, and the requisite ghosts from the past. . . . Duncan's off-hand treatment of romance allows her to focus on the intelligence and rationality of her heroine. The result is highly original; a gothic novel that is more a commentary on the dangers of education than on the perils of unrequited love."[5]

Summer of Fear

Summer of Fear, published in 1976, tells another page-turning adventure of the occult, this time featuring satanism, or black witchcraft. Rachel's happy life is suddenly changed when her cousin Julia is introduced to the family circle after a car accident kills her parents. Rachel tries to like Julia, but there is something disturbing about her. In fact, when Rachel first meets Julia she is struck particularly by her eyes, which "were deep and dark and filled with secrets. Haunted eyes. Haunting eyes. They were the strangest eyes I had ever seen."[6]

Rachel is fifteen; Julia is two years older. Rachel's family lives in Albuquerque; Julia's lived in the Ozarks. But it is not the difference in age and background that make Rachel uneasy, it is Julia herself. Julia's eyes continue to bother Rachel, for they "bored into me with such intensity that they gave me a feeling of having been caught and pinned in place by a physical force. . . . It was a strange feeling being studied so intently" (*Summer*, 35). It's not just Julia's eyes, either. Rachel's dog, Trickle, doesn't like Julia. The usually friendly pet growls in her presence and later bites her in the ankle.

At first Rachel seems to be the only one of her friends and family that is unsettled by Julia. In fact, Rachel's older brother, Pete, seems fascinated by the plain young woman, describing her as beautiful. Rachel's best friend, Carolyn, expresses a liking for Julia, and her father likes Julia almost too much. Then when Rachel comes down with hives just before the big dance, her boyfriend Mike finds he likes Julia too much, too.

To make things worse, Rachel begins to have problems with her mother. With Julia becoming accepted by everyone, Rachel begins to feel as if she's the odd person out in many ways. Frustrated, Rachel snoops in Julia's things and finds strange items, such as a peculiar wax effigy. When Rachel's dog Trickle dies, Rachel's dislike for Julia turns to hatred. In her sadness and concern, Rachel turns to Professor Jarvis, a retired neighbor who once taught sociology. He assures Rachel that evil witches do exist, and Rachel reads up on witchcraft at the library. Impressed by her newly discovered information, Rachel confronts Julia, accusing her of being a witch. Professor Jarvis has a stroke, and Rachel is sure that somehow Julia is responsible. To top things off, Rachel starts to discover clues that suggest Julia is an impostor.

Rachel's mother, a photographer, has been using Julia as a model. One day when her mother is away, Rachel discovers Julia spoiling negatives and realizes she's doing so because witches cannot be photographed. Julia is trying to destroy the evidence that would surely implicate her as a witch: she is not in the photographs for which she has posed. Julia admits to Rachel that she is really Sarah Blane, her family's servant girl. It had been thought that Sarah was killed in the car accident, but the girl that had been killed was Julia. Sarah took Julia's identity, and snatched at a chance for a better life and an opportunity to practice her witchcraft arts in a wider geographical area. Sarah taunts Rachel and claims that she will kill Rachel's mother and take Rachel's father for her husband.

In a dramatic climax, Rachel saves her mother from the car accident that Julia/Sarah has arranged, and the witch disappears from Rachel's life. Rachel's family life returns to normal. She gets Mike back as a boyfriend, but she occasionally reads and hears of strange happenings in the area and wonders if Julia/Sarah is still at work as a witch.

One reader of *Summer of Fear* wrote to Duncan about her reaction to the book. "I just finished reading *Summer of Fear,* and you do not know how shocked I was. Your book really made me appreciate my mother. After I had stopped shaking I went over and hugged her, which is something I had not done in a long time." (Edwards speech)

To date, *Summer of Fear* is the only book by Duncan to have been made into a movie. Retitled *Stranger in Our House,* it was first aired on Halloween evening, 1978, on NBC. The movie was directed by Wes Craven, a successful director of many horror films noted for playing up confrontations between good and evil, as exemplified in this case by the two girls. The film starred Linda Blair, who played a young girl possessed by the devil in the 1973 blockbuster *The Exorcist.* At the time the movie was being made, Duncan's daughter, Kerry Arquette, was in Hollywood attempting a career as an actress. Purely by coincidence, she landed a bit part in the film.

The movie plot retains most of the events of Duncan's book, although the dog Trickle is changed to a horse named Sundance. According to an interview Duncan gave, this change was made because the star, Linda Blair, liked horses.[7] At any rate, it is far more visually dramatic to have a rearing horse attack the cowering Julia than having a dog nip at her ankle.

In the *Times Literary Supplement,* Jennifer Moody singles out Duncan's narrative skills in this title. "The slow revelation of Julia's propensities raises this tale above inconsequential narrative. . . . The development of the narrative is steady, and tension is maintained admirably. Suitably baffling clues are dropped throughout and pulled together deftly in the final resolution of the mystery. Characters are rounded, believable and, with the exception of the dastardly Julia, lovable."[8]

Stranger with My Face

Laurie Stratton is the protagonist of *Stranger with My Face,* another popular Duncan story with a psychic theme. Laurie has

Left: A horrified Rachel stares at the deranged face in the mirror in the ominous 1977 paperback cover for *Summer of Fear,* first published in 1976. Right: Probably the same artist designed the 1982 paperback cover for *Stranger with My Face,* first publshed in 1981. Here, Laurie glances over her shoulder, catching the elusive visage of her mysterious doppelgänger, evil twin Lia. *Credit: Cam Chasteen*

been living a pleasant life with her family, and enjoying new found popularity with her handsome boyfriend, Gordon. Then something peculiar happens: someone who looks just like Laurie enters her life and begins to affect her in a strange, unsettling way. She doesn't know what to make of this doppelgänger, but somehow she senses that this shadow-self is her own twin sister, Lia, from whom she had been separated at birth.

Laurie confronts her parents about her background, and they confirm her suspicion that she was adopted and has an identical twin sister. Laurie is half Native American, which explains her dark coloring. Laurie's new friend from the Southwest, Helen, tells Laurie about some Navaho customs, in particular the ability of some people to involve themselves in astral projection, or out-of-body experiences, a way to leave the body and move about the world at will.

Laurie's shadow-self Lia tries to teach Laurie astral projection. Laurie is not unduly suspicious of Lia at first. Then Helen is attacked and lies comatose in a hospital. Laurie's romance with Gordon breaks up, and she begins a new friendship with Jeff, who was once handsome but was terribly scarred in an accident.

Laurie realizes at last that Lia has a purpose in finding her, and that purpose is a foul one. Lia is not only responsible for Helen's condition, but also for trying to kill Jeff and Laurie. Lia takes over Laurie's body when Laurie is on an astral projection journey. In her astral trips, Laurie discovers that Lia had caused the death of her foster sister and has been confined to a mental institution. Laurie is saved in the end by Jeff and her sister Megan, who confront the impostor. They break the astral cord, and Laurie is able to return to her own body. In the end, Laurie finds out that Lia's body had "died" and was cremated, yet Laurie senses that the astral spirit of Lia, her sister, will be with her forever.

One author who has written about the phenomena of out-of-body experiences, Janet Lee Mitchell, reports on psychical research in this area which tallies with Duncan's fictional descriptions: "Sensations of naturalness, completeness, reality, lightness, freedom, vitality, health, elations, and superiority are reported. A person will often react to an OBE [out-of-body experience] with surprise or fear or both. The fear usually results from lack of control of movements and the idea that one will not be able to get back into the body, in other words, fear of death."[9]

Duncan had talked with people who claimed to have experienced astral projection, which helped with her descriptions. She also did library research on the subject. The idea of astral projection appeals to many teen readers of this book. One wrote to Duncan, saying, "It would be so wonderful to have the power of astral projection. Don't get me wrong, I'm not discontented with my life as it is. I'm just absorbed by the ideas in this book. I've been trying to find out everything I can about the subject, and it's amazing all the research that's been done that nobody even knows about. There's so much more to life than I ever thought there was" (Edwards speech).

By reading Laurie's description of an out-of-body experience, one can understand the enthusiasm for this idea:

> Free in a world of sky! It stretched in all directions. I could rise into it, if I wished, and keep on rising. I could become part of it and expand beyond into nothing and everything. The evening air should have been cold, but I did not feel it. I could see straight through the gray clouds to the sun. Up I rose, until the clouds lay far behind me. The wind came singing, and it carried a million stories. Lia had been right, there were no words here. There did not have to be. All things were known and understood. A gull screamed somewhere miles away, and I knew. A child cried on the mainland, and I heard. I was apart from the earth, yet everything on it was mine.[10]

In *Stranger with My Face,* Duncan based the characters of Laurie's brother and sister on her children, Don Junior and Kaitlyn. As in a number of her books, Duncan adds little details from her own life that are fun to discover. For example, in *Stranger with My Face,* the name of an actress mentioned in passing is Kerry Arquette, the name of one of Duncan's daughters, who was an actress and television personality at that time. This seems almost prophetic in view of Kerry Arquette's role in the movie *Stranger in Our House.* In another place in the book, Helen is moved to Duke University hospital, where Duncan had taken her oldest daughter, Robin, for an operation.

Examination of Duncan's original manuscript and accompanying papers in the Kerlan Collection at the University of Minnesota provide a good example of how Duncan goes about providing details for her books. The setting of *Stranger with My Face* is a New England seacoast island in the fall. Duncan had been on Nantucket Island during the summer and sought information about seasonal changes on such an island. A cousin living in Rhode Island provided information for Duncan, who was then able to work in specific details throughout the book, such as:

> In the meanwhile, autumn moved in upon us. The air became crisp and then chill, and the trees on the mainland turned gold and red. On the island the grasses and sea oats browned. The little scrub oaks lost their leaves, and the poison ivy in the thickets along the sides of the road blazed a brilliant crimson.
>
> By mid-October the prams had been removed from the water, and the only boats to be seen upon the horizon were those of commercial fishermen. The souvenir shops and the art gallery closed, and the streets of the village were void of tourists. The waves curled high on the deserted beaches, and blue days alternated with gray. (*Stranger,* 76)

The reviewer for *Kirkus* referred to *Stranger with My Face* as one of Duncan's "sleazier supernatural thrillers,"[11] but other critics were complimentary. "One must, of course, suspend disbelief to accept the story, but Duncan makes it possible and palatable by a deft twining of fantasy and reality, by giving depth to characters and relationships, and by writing with perception and vitality about other, universal aspects of adolescent life as well as the more dramatic core of the story, a core that includes Laurie's discovery she is adopted."[12]

The Third Eye

Duncan often uses simple yet important themes in her books. In *The Third Eye,* such a theme might well be described in the words of the old axiom to thine own self be true. Karen, the eighteen-year-old psychic heroine, must come to terms with her special gift and help two important people in her life, her new boyfriend and her mother, to do the same.

At first Karen denies her psychic talents, for she is frightened by her ability to help find missing children and dislikes the publicity it generates. Her mother urges her to deny her gift, and a boy she is dating at the moment concludes she is a sort of freak. Yet

Karen cannot turn her back on the good that can be accomplished with her gift, and she eventually accepts responsibility for it. She helps her mother admit that she, too, has second sight, but has denied this talent for fear of being different. Karen's new boyfriend, a young police officer, also benefits by her gentle courage, for he comes to see the importance of doing what he wants to do rather than being content to play second fiddle to his seemingly more successful older brother.

As reported in Duncan's later true-crime book, *Who Killed My Daughter?*, Duncan believes a character in *The Third Eye* was a premonition of a psychic detective she was to consult after her daughter Kaitlyn's death. When Duncan first saw Betty Muench, she immediately remembered the description of the fictional psychic detective Anne Summers in *The Third Eye:* "The woman who lay in the bed on the far side of it was singularly unremarkable in appearance. She had a round, pleasant face, wide-spaced hazel eyes that seemed to be struggling to focus, and a mouth that was a bit too large to synchronize with her other features. The hair that lay spread across the pillow was chestnut color and lightly frosted with gray."[13] Betty Muench looks very similar.

Karen is without a doubt one of the most likeable of Duncan's characters. She is courageous and good, yet her gentle vulnerability and shyness make her appealing rather than a goody-two-shoes. Her policeman boyfriend, Ron, is also genuine, earnest without being sanctimonious. The reader is pleased when romance strikes, for they seem to be two nice people who deserve each other. The reviewer for *Voice of Youth Advocates,* Elaine Martindall, enthusiastically endorsed this book for the Best Books List, saying, "A fast read that will be a sure fire success with many readers."[14]

Locked in Time

The last of Duncan's books to use an occult theme is *Locked in Time.* Based on a "what-if" premise—Duncan wondered what it would be like if her thirteen-year-old daughter never grew out of that terrible age—*Locked in Time* blends the horror of the occult with real-life threats of murder and death:

> The idea . . . originated when the youngest of my five children turned 13. Overnight my darling Kate changed from an adorable cherub who thought her mother was perfect into a hostile teenager who thought everything about Mother, from her hairstyle to her "dumb jokes," was "utterly gross." My husband tried to comfort me by saying, "It's just a phase all adolescents go through. Our other kids outgrew it, and so will Kate."
>
> The Mother part of me knew that he was right.
>
> The Writer part of me whispered—"What if she doesn't?"
>
> What if a mother and her adolescent daughter were locked in time? What would it be like to live for all eternity with a hostile, rebellious 13-year-old who never outgrew her training bra—who never got rid of her acne—and who knew that I, her mother, was responsible for that situation?
>
> Once I'd gotten that far in my thinking, I was racing for the typewriter. (DD pamphlet, 2)

Nore (short for Eleanor) Robbins arrives in Louisiana to meet her new stepfamily. Her mother had been killed in an accident, and Nore's father has remarried. His new wife is Lisette, a widow with two children: Gabe, who is Nore's age, seventeen, and Josie, thirteen. There had once been another son, Louis, who was killed riding a wild stallion.

Nore finds Shadow Grove, the old plantation in the bayous, very different from upstate New York and New England. The isolated setting forces her to learn quickly about her new family. She feels uneasy from the beginning and is led to believe that things are not quite right at Shadow Grove. Though she is rather taken with Gabe, who is handsome, and comes to like Josie very much, she resents Lisette, partly because she doesn't like the idea of a replacement of her own beloved mother.

Nore begins to wonder about comments that Gabe and Josie make, and the odd relationship between them and their mother, Lisette. There is definitely something askew, something mysterious, about Nore's new family. The only note of normalcy, apart from her author father, is Dave Parlange, a local teen who is helping his uncle repair the roof of the decaying old plantation house.

Nore discovers a number of clues to make her even more suspicious. She finds an old photograph of people who look exactly like Lisette, Gabe, and Josie. Things come to a head when Gabe rejects Nore after initially indicating that he is attracted to her. After a brooding spell, he invites her to go out into the bayous with him in an old boat. He deliberately tries to drown Nore, who cannot swim. She miraculously saves herself and returns to Shadow Grove. Her accusations are not believed, and her sense of frustration and fear about the mysteries of Shadow Grove intensify. She breaks into a locked slave cabin used for storage and discovers many papers, including Lisette's journals. At last the mystery is solved.

As a young wife and mother nearly a century earlier, Lisette had made a pact with a voodoo priestess. She had learned the secret of stopping the aging process for herself and her children. The attempt was successful, except for Louis, who had deliberately tempted fate and was killed by a wild horse. In Gabe's words, "sixty-nine years of childhood was enough."[15] Nore's father is leaving on a business trip to New York and doesn't have time to listen to Nore's story. Nore tries to escape but is captured by Lisette, who locks her in the old cabin with Dave, who has tried to help Nore. Lisette sets the cabin on fire, but at the last minute they are saved by Josie. Lisette and Gabe die in a car accident, probably suicides, and Nore is left with Josie, who will always be thirteen years old.

Duncan's skill as a writer is amply demonstrated in this fast-paced, exciting story. In addition to an original premise and well-constructed plot, she is able to get inside some of her characters and give the reader a chance to consider viewpoints other than Nore's. *Locked in Time* is a first-person narrative, yet we grow to understand the motivations of characters besides the protagonist. The following brief and poignant comment made by Josie helps tell the story from another point of view: "Friends grow away from you and they *do* die! That's why it's better not to get too attached to people. When you do, all that happens is that you end up sad" (*Locked,* 90).

In this story, Duncan uses the idea of a vivid grief dream, based on the sensations she had experienced after the death of her mother. Duncan's dream reassured her that her mother's spirit still existed after death. Nore's dream is not the same in its message, but it is still powerful:

> A hand touched my cheek, and when, in the dream, my eyes flew open, it was to find my mother standing by my bedside.
>
> I was not surprised. I had such dreams quite often.
>
> "Mother," I said, "what are you doing here? You're supposed to be *dead!*"
>
> "Not to you," the familiar voice said matter-of-factly. "I'm not dead to *you*, Nore. Now listen, because I have something important to tell you. I want you to repack your things and leave Shadow Grove immediately." . . .
>
> "By September, it will be too late," my mother told me. "You and your father are both in terrible danger. You must talk to Dad, you must tell him—*Nore are you listening?*
>
> But, I wasn't any longer. Caught in the tides of sleep, I was drifting away from her, and the shreds of blowing cotton were becoming a snowstorm. The branches of the oak trees were dipping lower and lower, and their leaves were sending shadows flickering across the fading image of Mother's face. (*Locked,* 22)

Often when writers become known for certain popular books, they are reviewed more frequently. This has been true for Duncan, although it has not meant necessarily that her books have received more in-depth analysis of themes and style. Rather, the reviews consist mainly of plot summaries. In the case of *Locked in Time*, however, most of the reviews tended to dwell on the southern gothic characteristics of the setting, while still predicting popularity for the title. One reviewer at least, Sarah Hayes, looked beyond these superficial details and commented on Duncan's skill as a storyteller: "The growing sense of unease is Lois Duncan's hallmark. . . . She can play the part of the novelist, but at heart she is a spine-chiller. Her stories are not literary, or particularly stylish or complex: just readable, compelling and very frightening."[16]

Duncan is primarily thought of by teachers and librarians as a writer of occult thrillers. The scary aspects of the supernatural do jump quickly to mind when considering the body of Duncan's work for teens. In fact, the authors of a standard text on young adult literature, Kenneth L. Donelson and Alleen Pace Nilsen, comment only on this aspect of Duncan's work, without consideration for some of her other popular titles, such as *Killing Mr. Griffin*. "*Stranger with My Face* and *The Third Eye* were enjoyable but hardly added to Duncan's luster after *Summer of Fear*. *Locked in Time*, however, is as spooky as *Summer of Fear* and in some ways superior to the earlier book."[17]

At various times in her career, Lois Duncan has been charged with misusing her talent. Critics occasionally term her writing "slick" and want her gifts turned to more literary pursuits. These criticisms, however, have decreased in recent years, no doubt because of adults' relief at seeing kids read anything at all, even thrillers. Certainly, one cannot fault Duncan for her storytelling skill. It would seem reasonable to argue with Duncan's critics and suggest that teens have the right to read exciting books for fun, and they deserve them to be well written.

5. *Killing Mr. Griffin*

One of Lois Duncan's most popular young adult thrillers is *Killing Mr. Griffin* (1978). It is sandwiched between *Summer of Fear* (1976), an occult thriller featuring a witch girl, and *Daughters of Eve* (1979), Duncan's most controversial book, dealing with touchy feminist issues.

Killing Mr. Griffin, however, deals with neither supernatural nor social concerns. It is the dream of many teenagers come true, a fantasy revenge story in which some youngsters, under the spell of a charismatic classmate, try to take control of a situation. Their scheme unravels, and they must eventually face the consequences of their actions.

As with *Ransom,* the earlier thriller by Duncan, there are five major teenage characters, again three boys and two girls. The undisputed leader of the group is Mark, an unprincipled and persuasive senior who lives with his aunt and uncle, who seldom see him and seem relieved that he will soon be eighteen and independent of them. Mark's closest friend is Jeff, a basketball star who finds Mark intriguing. Jeff's girlfriend, Betsy, is a cute, bouncy cheerleader who secretly yearns for Mark's attentions. The threesome draft David Ruggles, a sensitive boy who is president of the senior class, and Sue McConnell, a mousey, awkward girl with creative talent who strives to gain A grades from their despised English teacher, Mr. Griffin. Mark has reasoned that two "good" students are necessary for the success of his plan.

In an interview, Duncan explained that the character of Mr. Griffin was based on one of her daughter's English teachers, a woman. Duncan changed the gender of the teacher so as not to embarrass the model. The action starts at Del Norte High School in Albuquerque, where Duncan's children attended school (RDA interview). Although the character of Mr. Griffin was based on a real person, he is also an archetype; most people can remember a teacher like him, a perfectionist, a martinet who is never satisfied with his students' work.

Behind the scenes, however, we learn about Mr. Griffin's motivation. He is a former college professor who has decided it is essential to reach students at an earlier age if they are to learn. He married late in life, and in his early forties, he and his wife are expecting their first child. Seen through his wife's loving eyes, Mr. Griffin becomes understandable, even sympathetic for maintaining his high-minded goals.

As Duncan has stated, "I liked the character of Mr. Griffin. Looking at my own children, I realized that some of the demanding teachers that they couldn't stand when they were in school were later, when they grew up, teachers they remembered with great affection and gratitude, because those were the teachers who had made the biggest difference in their lives. I wanted Mr. Griffin to be one of those teachers, symbolic of that kind of teacher—one of the ones who aren't appreciated at the time but later are."[1]

Contrasted with the students who object to Mr. Griffin's rigorous approach, he seems admirable in some ways. His wife trys to persuade him to be kinder and more considerate to his students, to be more encouraging of them. The reader thinks that perhaps she is making some headway.

"It was a wild, windy, southwestern spring when the idea of killing Mr. Griffin occurred to them."[2] This gripping first sentence grabs and holds the readers' interest in the story, and it takes a while to set the stage for the action decided upon by the frustrated teens. Their frustration has been building for some time. Sue, used to getting high grades, is discouraged by the B's and C's she receives from Mr. Griffin. Mark has been forced to repeat the class because he plagiarized a term paper, and Mr. Griffin made him beg to be readmitted to the class. Basketball star Jeff, a senior hoping to graduate, is given no concessions on deadlines, even if a big game is scheduled for the night a difficult bit of homework is assigned. Betsy agrees with Mark on everything. Even conscientious David is upset, having received an F for an assignment that blew away in the wild wind, since Mr. Griffin refuses to accept anything late.

It is Mark, of course, who comes up with the idea. He suggests that Mr. Griffin needs a good scare from his students to teach him a lesson and earn them respect. Mark convinces the others that they should kidnap Mr. Griffin. As he points out, students had "mock kidnapped" Dolly Luna, a popular teacher, the year before, and it had all been viewed as great fun by everyone involved. Mark explains that if anything goes awry, they can always claim they were simply emulating the stunt of the year before, and besides, since they are all minors, they need not fear harsh punishment.

The other four agree, some more enthusiastically than others, to kidnap Mr. Griffin, take him to a deserted spot in the mountains, and leave him overnight, giving him a good scare. This experience should make the hated teacher more understanding and tolerant, they reason.

David is reluctant about the plan, but decides to go along with it. Sue, who will be the decoy, has to be talked into it, but she is so desperate for acceptance and friendship from the other more popular students, that she agrees to the scheme. She makes an appointment to see Mr. Griffin about her classwork after school.

The actual kidnapping goes as planned, with careful alibis established. The only complication is created by Betsy, who is stopped for speeding and given a ticket. At the last minute, Sue refuses to go to the mountains with the others, overcome with guilt. Since her most essential part in the plot is already accomplished, the rest leave her behind as they head for their secret picnic place.

Mr. Griffin is courageous and does not grovel before his kidnappers. It has been established earlier that he has a heart condition and must take medication when under stress, but the students pay little attention to the medicine vial when it falls from the teacher's pocket. Because of his unrepentant attitude, the teens leave him tightly bound and blindfolded, expecting that he will be more pliable in the morning after a night exposed to the cold.

Later that evening, David and Sue decide to rescue Mr. Griffin. Sue is especially guilt-ridden, since the last thing Mr. Griffin did in the school parking lot as he was tackled from behind was to warn her to run. He obviously had concern for her safety, even as he was being captured.

When David and Sue reach the picnic place in the mountains, they are horrified to find that Mr. Griffin is dead. They return to town and tell the others of their discovery. Mark assures them that he'll take care of everything so they won't get caught. He is emphatic about keeping the kidnapping scheme a secret.

The next day, Mrs. Griffin reports her husband missing. Sue is summoned from class to be questioned. Mark, planning to make it look like the teacher has deserted his pregnant wife, has told Sue to say she saw a young blond woman in Mr. Griffin's car waiting for him.

After school, Mark, Jeff, Betsy, and David go back to the scene of the crime to bury Mr. Griffin. David steals Mr. Griffin's class ring from Stanford University, where David's own father had gone to college—a man who had deserted the family years earlier. Betsy drives Mr. Griffin's car to the airport parking lot, where she is spotted by the same officer who had given her a speeding ticket the day before. Then the body is discovered, an event triggered by casual lovers finding the lost pill vial.

By this time, the students are extremely nervous. Sue spends most of her time weeping out of guilt and fear, but Jeff and Betsy feel no remorse for their part in the deed. They have convinced themselves that all they meant to do was give Mr. Griffin a good scare, and that Mark will see them through this sticky time. Mark continues to plot and connive; he is the only one not afraid of being caught.

Mrs. Griffin tries to get Sue to tell the truth about her last moments with the teacher. Betsy tells Mark about the problem with her alibi. Mark decides to retrieve Mr. Griffin's car from the airport parking lot, have Jeff repaint it, then abandon it on a remote Indian reservation.

David has hidden the Stanford ring in his drawer. His grand-mother discovers it there, and refuses to give it back. He tells Mark, who says he'll take care of it. Events are building toward the climax.

Sue is left out of the action, and the others hope she will keep her mouth shut. Mark kills David's grandmother to get the ring. Finally, Mark waits until Sue is home alone. He ties her up and sets the house on fire. Fortunately, Mrs. Griffin arrives at Sue's house in the nick of time. She has come determined to force Sue to tell the truth.

In the end, Mark is revealed for the psychopath he really is. He will probably be tried for murder. Jeff, David, and Betsy face criminal charges for manslaughter—their status as minors did not protect them at all—and Sue will probably get off lightly by turning state's evidence. Mrs. Griffin gives the girl her last graded assignment for Mr. Griffin, which includes encouraging com-ments—just what guilt-ridden Sue needs!

Peer Pressure and Teens

In *Killing Mr. Griffin,* Duncan explores a theme she uses many times in her work: the importance of standing up for one's own beliefs. Although the character of Sue and the situation she finds herself in are delineated in an extreme way, she serves as a sym-bol of good as opposed to the unscrupulous, criminal Mark.

Teens and peer pressure have been studied, written about, and discussed in many places. The following letter from the "Dear Abby" column, from Ms. J. Benson of San Diego, does a good job of describing peer pressure in action:

> I recall vividly back in the '60s as a teenager when a bunch of my friends and I were hanging out in my best friend's garage, pass-ing around the community cigarette. I passed it to a girl named Sandy and she said, "No thanks, I don't smoke."

Left: An early (1979) paperback cover for *Killing Mr. Griffin* shows four frightened teens looking down at the body of their English teacher. From the circumstances and descriptions in the book, they are probably, from left to right, David, Betsy, Mark, and Jeff. The updated cover (1990), in keeping with the other book covers from the same period, shows only the feet of the corpse with a rope entwined around the ankles. *Credit: Cam Chasteen*

> I remember thinking that she was so brave and independent for refusing to smoke when peer pressure was so great, but to go along with crowd, I joined in and razzed her for being a "Miss Goody-Goody." I often wish that I had been as independent as she was, because I am now battling a 25-year addiction to cigarettes. . . .
>
> I still hold a great deal of respect for her, even though she never knew how I really felt, and I haven't seen her in 25 years.[3]

Teens are particularly vulnerable to peer pressure. Being part of a popular group of people, belonging, being approved of by the right gang—all this is important in building self-esteem, something that tends to be very fragile in the adolescent years. Sue Mc-

Connell is a victim of Mark's calculating attempt to get what he wanted. Mark is a master of manipulation, and peer pressure is just one of the techniques he employs.

The Character of Mark

The character of Mark is based on one of Duncan's daughter's boyfriends, as she explains:

> Sometimes it is a personality that triggers a plot idea. One of our daughters had a nearly disastrous love affair with a strange and frightening young man. I used to lie awake nights, listening to police and ambulance sirens going by on the freeway, praying that she would come home safe from her date.
>
> Something was wrong with that boy. I knew it. Don knew it. But we couldn't pinpoint what it was. Our daughter knew it too, but was too infatuated to break away. Eventually something occurred that forced her to realize that she had to. It was not until much later that she could bring herself to discuss the relationship and to reveal to us the sort of person the boy had been.
>
> I thought, thank God, he's out of our lives!
>
> But he wasn't—quite. His memory stayed with me, and later, when I was taking a class in abnormal psychology, I found him in a text book. There was a detailed description complete with a clinical name. I began to do some reading about this personality disorder and to discuss it with a friend who was a psychologist. I wanted to understand how such a person could have so much influence over others. Finally, I wrote a book called *Killing Mr. Griffin* in which a boy named "Mark" is instrumental in causing the death of his English teacher. Mark bears no outward resemblance to my daughter's former boyfriend. They are different people entirely. But, without having known the one, I would never have been able to create the other. (*How,* 189)

In *Killing Mr. Griffin,* Sue's mother explains Mark's immorality to her daughter by reading from a textbook:

> "'This individual has a behavior pattern that brings him repeatedly into conflict with society. He is incapable of significant loy-

alty to individuals, groups or social values. He is selfish, callous, irresponsible, impulsive and totally unable to experience guilt. His frustration level is low; he cannot stand to be thwarted. He tends to blame others or offer plausible rationalizations for his behavior.'"

She paused. "Sound familiar?"

When Susan did not answer, her mother continued. "'There's more. This individual is unique among pathological personalities in appearing, even on close examination, to be not only quite normal but unusually intelligent and charming. He appears quite sincere and loyal and may perform brilliantly at any endeavor. He often has a tremendous charismatic power over others.'

Now do you recognize someone?"

"It's a description of Mark," Susan said.

"It's a clinical description of a psychopath." (*Killing*, 219–20)

The charismatic nature of this personality type is well illustrated in *Killing Mr. Griffin*. When Jeff, who could have been a sympathetic character, remembers how he first became friends with Mark—they set fire to a live cat—the reader quickly dismisses Jeff as a sycophant. Even David, who is not a close friend of Mark's, can only think of turning to him for help when he and Sue discover Mr. Griffin's body. Sue wants to go to her dad, but David has only one thought in his head: *"We've got to get to Mark. Mark will know what to do"* (*Killing*, 219–20). Mark does indeed know what to do, but his schemes to wiggle out of this complication rather than face up to the awful situation lead to disaster.

Sue and David

The two most sympathetic teen characters in the book, and the two people the reader spends most time with as the plot unfolds, are Sue and David. One cannot help but wonder if Duncan has split the role of sympathetic protagonist into two people, one of each gender, to ensure readership from both boys and girls.

Sue is shy and kind at heart. Some of her personality traits are reminiscent of Duncan's descriptions of herself as a very young teen. Sue is not pretty and sparkling. She wears glasses

(Duncan had braces) and loves to write, including poetry. The unfortunate thing about Sue is that while she has reason for her tears, her fears, and her guilty conscience, she's not much of a fighter. She lacks backbone and spirit. It's no wonder the others have no time for "a little creep with glasses" (*Killing*, 23). Sue's vulnerability makes her sympathetic, even pitiable, to the reader, but she comes across in the end as something of a coward. The reader has some pity for her, as does David, who reflects, "There was no reason for a girl like Susan to be here, frightened and remorseful, staggering around the mountain darkness. Why had he drawn her into this crazy plot? he asked himself angrily" (*Killing*, 99).

David, on the other hand, is an interesting character. He lives with his mother and grandmother, who is frail and housebound. David is portrayed as a sensitive boy, kind to his grandmother, although the drudgery of reporting home every day to attend to her needs would drive most teens to rebellion. He feels some irritation over his mother's self-imposed martyrdom, yet sympathizes with her situation. He does seem a bit calculating in his determination to get a college scholarship and ultimately become a lawyer, but he is constantly reminded by his mother that he will someday have to be the family's mainstay.

In spite of their seemingly higher sense of morality, Sue and David are susceptible to Mark's charm. Sue thinks:

> When Mark told you something, you did it. She could understand now what David had meant when he had told her, "Mark isn't like other people." There was a strength in Mark, an ability to know exactly what to do in any emergency, and when Mark said something, you had to believe it, because if you couldn't believe in Mark, you couldn't believe in anything. "Trust me— trust old Mark," he had told her last night, his arms a comforting fortress around her. "Everything's going to be all right."
> Mark knew; he *had* to know. If they did exactly what he told them, things would somehow work out and the terrible present would one day lie behind them and be the past, and people could forget the past if they tried to. But it was important, terribly important, to do precisely as Mark said. (*Killing*, 129)

Reactions to *Killing Mr. Griffin*

Duncan describes an extreme reaction to *Killing Mr. Griffin* as a result of a censor misunderstanding:

> The teacher had just said, "Open your books" when five men in business suits burst into a junior high school classroom in Colorado where students were reading and discussing a novel, *Killing Mr. Griffin*. The men tore down the bulletin board on which the book jacket was displayed, and ripped copies of the book out of the students' hands. The reason? Not having read the book, the men assumed from the title that it was a Mafia-inspired guide book for murder. . . .
>
> In the case of *Killing Mr. Griffin*, the book was being used as a springboard for a class discussion about the dangers involved in knuckling under to peer pressure and the need to take responsibility for one's own actions.[4]

Another censorship attempt on *Killing Mr. Griffin*, this time in California, was reported in the *Newsletter on Intellectual Freedom*. In this case, parents of a sixth-grade boy complained when a report on the book was assigned to the students in Sinnott Elementary School in Milpitas, California. The mother, Mary Toller-Collins, requested immediate removal of the book because it contained "needlessly foul" language and had no "redeeming qualities."[5] David Collins, the father, said, "It had no moral for young minds. There was no clear message other than a very vague reference about not succumbing to peer pressure" (Milpitas, 123). In spite of the complaints at both the school and public libraries, the book was retained in Milpitas, where the book review committee said in its report that the plot "was well-constructed and holds the reader's interest," and that values were "clearly stated" (Milpitas, 123).

When *Killing Mr. Griffin* was first published it received mixed reviews. It was praised for its "skillful plotting [which] builds layers of tension," and "the ending is nicely handled in a manner which provides relief without removing any of the chilling implications."[6] Yet Duncan's slickness as a writer was hinted at, and some reviews, expressed uneasiness with the story itself.

Killing Mr. Griffin was read enthusiastically by teens from the time of its publication and remains a favorite today. It is frequently used in classrooms as a vehicle for discussion about teenage peer pressure. The book has been awarded readers' choice awards in three states; Alabama, California, and Massachusetts. The American Library Association named *Killing Mr. Griffin* a "Best of the Best Books for Young Adults" in 1978. The citation for the Margaret A. Edwards Award in 1992 cites *Killing Mr. Griffin* as one of Lois Duncan's most important works.

A letter to Duncan from one student tells about his reactions to the book. "Our class just finished reading *Killing Mr. Griffin*. Our teacher asked us, 'Do you think Susan was guilty?' A lot of the kids said, 'No, because she wasn't even there when they tied the guy up.' But my answer was, 'I think Susan was just as guilty as the others because she knew what her friends were going to do, and she didn't do anything about it" (Edwards speech).

One reviewer commented that the book was "skillfully written and fast-moving." But the same critic went on to say, "Though the author tells a convincing story, her characters are highly stereotyped, and the fact that she deals with questions of responsibility and integrity on such a superficial level and in such a slick way is particularly disturbing. Above all, the inclusion of so much malevolence seems unjustified."[7]

In the *New York Times Book Review,* Richard Peck, a respected young adult novelist, commended Duncan for her original idea and remarked that "the value of the book lies in the twisted logic of the teen-agers and how easily they can justify anything." He then went on to say, "But the plot descends into unadultered melodrama. One murder leads to another. And a murder attempt at the end is evidently meant to establish the comparative innocence of one character at the expense of the others. The book becomes 'an easy' when it shouldn't. But there's veracity unto the end: the parents are the last to lose their innocence." The final paragraph of the review predicts a lack of readership for the book, since "teen-agers won't choose to identify with these meticulously unflattering portrayals, though they'll see their friends in them."[8]

In spite of Peck's criticisms about her book, Duncan considers him a good friend today. She tells of their first meeting:

After I had written *Killing Mr. Griffin*, Richard Peck reviewed it for *The New York Times*. I read his review, and he said some things in there I didn't remember having done. I went back and reread my book again, and I said, "Oh, Richard Peck, he knew exactly what he was doing." I had never met Richard Peck. Also, I think he had pointed out some weaknesses, and then I realized they were the same weaknesses he had in *Are You in the House Alone?* Of course he understood. From then on, I just wanted to meet Richard Peck.

I was asked to give a talk in Pennsylvania. . . . I saw Richard Peck was going to speak there, so I said I'd do it. I got there, did my stint, and looking around—nobody looked like Richard Peck. Finally, I was told he had broken his ankle that morning and hadn't been able to come. George Nicholson, our editor, was going to give Richard's talk. I was so disappointed.

George and I went back to New York together on the train, and George asked me to have dinner that night before going back to Albuquerque. I said, "Yes." George and I got to this restaurant and were eating dinner, and I looked up and there was this tall man on crutches with a bag of books over his shoulder. He comes limping across the room. I stand.

I said, "Richard Peck." And we moved towards each other. It was like television slow motion.

I said, "Richard Peck!"

He said, "Lois Duncan! Long have I loved you."

He had brought all his books autographed for me, and he had limped in just to have dinner with George and me. We've been fast friends ever since. (CK interview)

6. *Daughters of Eve*

Daughters of Eve is one of the most controversial of Lois Duncan's books. Ironically, it seems that Duncan did not write the book to cause a stir, but rather used the issue of feminism as a theme to highlight some of the same concerns she had written about before, such as encouraging teens to trust their better instincts and resisting influence by manipulators. In this story, the manipulator is not a teen like Mark in *Killing Mr. Griffin*, but an adult and a teacher.

When *Daughters of Eve* was published in 1979, feminism was as controversial a subject as it is today. Any social movement is bound to generate extreme attitudes and high emotions. There are seldom easy and quick solutions when social change and human beliefs are involved, and sometimes controversy is unintentionally triggered by events such as the publication of a book for teens. Duncan has never considered herself an ardent feminist, in spite of her early brushes with sexism, particularly as that affected her status on the high school newspaper. Duncan was told by a journalism teacher that the editor-in-chief was always a boy. Duncan did not fight this decision and found she enjoyed being the managing editor. She explains:

I got to do more as managing editor. It was before the age that you began thinking about things like women's lib. The first time I ever heard the term I thought, "How strange, equality for women." Because I thought as women we were equal. Since I never held a job outside the home. I never thought about it as being about difference in pay; I was never exposed to that kind of thing. The only job I had held paid little, but I thought I wasn't worth more than that. I didn't know what any of the men were being paid, so I didn't have anything to compare it to, so I was not a feminist at all. (CK interview)

Duncan has said that she feels fortunate in having chosen a career where there has not been major discrimination against women. She said, "It hasn't affected me greatly because I feel that my writing as far as I have known, has been treated fairly" (CK interview). She acknowledges, however, that her writing has been in traditional women's areas, and that some other genres of authorship might have been more difficult for her to enter, such as journalism or science fiction.

Duncan's personal view of feminism is rather middle-of-the-road, as the following illustrates:

Some feminists have protested books that contain statements they construe as sexist. One such book, one of my childhood favorites, is the Newbery-Medal-winning classic *Caddie Woodlawn*, published in 1935. Today's activists, worried about sexual stereotyping, term it a "footbinder" because it contains a scene in which a frontier child is advised by her father to stop acting like a tomboy. On the other side of the issue stand all books that portray women in any role other than that of contented housewife. ("Diary," 93)

At the time Duncan was writing *Daughters of Eve*, her own two older daughters were in their late teens.

At that point I knew they were going through some very difficult times. They thought that they were going to have it all—work at very wonderful careers, and at the same time they had this nesting instinct. They wanted to have babies. . . . They were pulled in all directions, thinking they should be able to do everything and not being able to. I began to see the problems that were facing young people. There were no longer any sexual guidelines for them. When I was growing up, you knew what you were supposed to do. They were being told they could go out and have the same kind of free sex men had. And yet they were finding out the men didn't want to marry them. . . . I remember one of my daughters coming home—she was living with her boyfriend—and she would come over with this big bag of laundry that she would do in my washing machine. She was keeping house, doing his laundry, plus paying her part of the rent. He wasn't even married to her, and he could walk out anytime he wanted to. . . . I couldn't see that all this wonderful freedom the girls were suddenly experiencing because of the feminist movement was working to their benefit one little bit. . . . (CK interview)

Duncan tells about the genesis of *Daughters of Eve* in *How to Write and Sell Your Personal Experiences:*

My editor at Little, Brown was enthusiastic about the idea [of a girl who gets involved in a religious cult]. I was too, initially, and then, as I wrote, I came to see that I was not prepared to take on such a project. I have never been involved in a religious cult, and neither, thank God, have any of my children. I couldn't make the cult leader generate the necessary charisma. The dialogue between him and his followers was flat and unnatural. Having no personal experiences upon which to draw, I had no straw to spin, and I had to let the project drop. The theme of the book—a persuasive adult asserting pressure upon the minds of vulnerable youngsters—stayed with me, however. Eventually I tried it again. This time I laid the story in the little Michigan town in which my husband Don was raised, and made the youth group a high school sorority and the adult an embittered man-hating woman teacher. Now I was on firm ground. I knew that teacher—and I knew the influence someone like her could have upon a group of young women (my daughters? my nieces?) struggling to find their places in a world of suddenly shifting values. The book came easily. I called it *Daughters of Eve*. (*How,* 207)

Duncan describes her editor's response to the new idea:

My editor warned me that I was walking on hot coals, and I thought, "He doesn't know what he's talking about." He knew exactly what he was talking about, because . . . all the feminists think it's an anti-feminist book, and all the anti-feminists think it's a feminist book. I liked the book. But I realized that these people felt so strongly they could not walk a line in the middle [of the feminist issue]. I was trying to walk with one foot on either side of a gray line by using ten different girls and showing all the benefits and all the other side of it. It didn't work that way. (CK interview)

Daughters of Eve tells the story of an exclusive high school girls' club, the Daughters of Eve. The primary focus of this book, however, unlike *Debutante Hill,* is not on elite cliques in high school. Instead, it presents a far more consequential problem for teens. One of the club's members, Tammy Carncross, daughter of Modesta High School's science teacher, has psychic premonitions, sometimes called second sight, or precognition. As the school year begins and the meetings of the club get under way with their new advisor, Irene Stark, Tammy is startled by a vision of blood on a white candle during the initiation ceremony for new members. She is sure that something terrible will happen and tentatively drops out of the club.

Otherwise, things seem fine. Amy becomes engaged to her boyfriend Dave, and plump Laura Snow secretly becomes involved with Peter. Peter is the selfish brother of another club member, Ruthie Grange, and former boyfriend of beautiful Bambi, also a club member and aspiring model who will not "put out" for Peter. Conflict arises when the club decides to donate their funds to help start a girls' soccer team rather than to support boys' athletics as in the past. The money is accepted by the administration of the school, but is given to the boys' basketball team in spite of the girls' wishes.

As the book evolves, Irene is revealed as a militant, embittered feminist, angry at being passed over for promotion on her previous job in favor of a less qualified man. Not only was she disappointed professionally, she felt personally betrayed because she had been romantically involved with the man. Laura becomes Peter's lover and is horrified later to discover that he was only using her for sex. She tries to commit suicide, but is thwarted in her attempt. She leaves Modesta to complete the school year in Rhode Island, where her father lives with his new family. Ann becomes pregnant, but does not give in automatically to Irene's suggestion she get an abortion, even though early marriage will mean sacrificing an art scholarship in Boston that Irene has arranged for her.

The club decides to take revenge on Peter for his callous seduction of Laura. They trap him late at night and shave off his handsome head of hair, which mortifies vain Peter. The club's president, Fran, competes in a science fair but is disqualified because of a regulation she had overlooked. Fran is disappointed yet accepting, but her sisters in the Daughters of Eve decide to avenge her. They wreak havoc in the science classroom, destroying some of Tammy's father's personal possessions in the process. Tammy then quits the club in earnest.

By this time the club membership has shrunk, but the core group decides not to take in any new members until the following year. Those remaining members, however, become even more attached to Irene. Jane Rheardon, for example, has found important support and escape in the club, and clings to the Daughters of Eve. She has a dreadful home life—her father beats her mother, who refuses to leave him. At one point Jane muses that "behind each door here [in Modesta] was a family, and every family held its own secrets, clutched tightly away from the eyes of the rest of the world. You didn't dishonor your family by discussing its problems with others."[1] This sad little reflection seems similar to the mother's denials in Judith Guest's *Ordinary People,* another novel of a dysfunctional family. This scene with Jane occurs early in the story and helps establish the sad circumstances of some of the girls. While Jane is thinking about her family in her room, her drunken father is down in the living room terrorizing Jane's mother, herself a former Daughter of Eve, into singing the club's secret song:

> But other people's fathers didn't get that wound up, did they? Did Ann Whitten's gentle, dreamy-faced father break character each Friday night to become a raging tyrant? . . .

I wish it were Monday, Jane thought wearily. I wish I were back in school again. Walking down the hall. People laughing and shoving. Lockers clanging. School smells. Chewing gum. Chalk. Tennis shoes. Peanut butter sandwiches and bananas.

Jane pressed her hands against the sides of her face to control the twitching. From the room below there came a thud and high-pitched cry.

A moment later in thin, wavering voice began to sing. (*Daughters*, 20)

Later, after Jane's mother is hospitalized with a broken hip, Jane moves in temporarily with Irene. When she returns home to get some clothes, her father, drunk, orders her to move back home and take on the role of housekeeper, and then, when her mother returns home, nurse.

"Don't you try telling me what I can and can't do, chicken." He picked up the newspaper which had fallen to the floor beside his chair and opened it to the sports section. "Go and fix us some dinner."

Jane stood, staring at him. "You want me to cook for you now?"

"Darned right, I do. With your mother out of commission, you're the lady of the house. You might as well start learning what woman's work is all about."

In the kitchen, her mother's heavy iron skillet stood in the drying rack. Jane picked it up and held it a moment, testing the weight of it. Then she went back into the living room, moving quietly, and stood behind her father's chair.

She lifted the skillet as high above her head as she was able. She closed her eyes. The smell of lemon-scented hair tonic filled her nostrils, and beneath it there was the faint, lingering odor of pipe tobacco. There was nothing of her mother. Nothing at all.

The left side of her face twitched violently.

With her eyes still closed, Jane braced herself and brought the skillet down with all her strength onto the top of her father's head. (*Daughters*, 293–94)

In a simple epilogue the fate of the book's characters is revealed. Some have married and settled into traditional roles as wives and mothers; some are in college. Ann did not have an abortion. Jane has been hospitalized for mental impairment, while Irene Stark has risen to the position of assistant principal of the high school.

An interesting and provocative subplot of *Daughters of Eve* is Tammy's precognition, the ability to sense the future. This phenomena has been noted world-wide and in many cultures. The gift of prophecy has been recorded in many ancient texts and handed down orally in many different societies.

Tammy's ability is somewhat erratic, true of many psychic talents, but she has learned to trust these premonitions in spite of some in the past that had not come true. During the induction ceremony for the Daughters of Eve, Tammy has the uneasy feeling she has come to recognize as a psychic premonition.

> Tammy herself could not remember that occasion, it was too far in her past, but over the years she had come to accept her "feelings" as a natural extension of her thought process. When she took a school exam, she would think through each problem to a logical answer, and then, before writing this down, she would ask herself, "but, what do I *feel?*" If the thought and the feeling were not compatible, she would redo the problem.
>
> Tammy also had feelings about people. These did not come to her often, but when they did occur they were rarely misleading. Two years ago she had been one of the girls standing before the row of candles, listening to the story of Ruth. . . .
>
> Today, with the same intensity of feeling, Tammy knew that something was very wrong. There was an alien presence in the room. It moved like a shadow between her eyes and the flickering candles, and though the room was warm, actually quite hot, . . . Tammy shivered. (*Daughters*, 29–30)

Discussions with Dr. William Roll of the Psychical Research Foundation following her daughter's murder led Lois Duncan to wonder if she herself had the gift of precognition. Dr. Roll told her that it is not uncommon for creative people to somehow know hints of future events and incorporate these into their writing. He gave her as an example a story written about the sinking of a mighty ship with detail eerily similar to the wreck of the *Titanic*—which occurred after the story's publication. Duncan may well

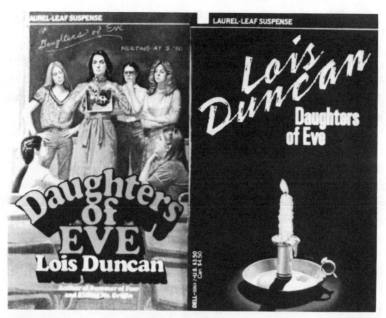

Left: An early (1980) paperback cover for *Daughters of Eve,* originally published in 1979. Judging from the descriptions in the book, the standing figures are probably Bambi, Irene Stark, Fran, and Jane. Seated may be Tammy and Laura. Right: The updated cover shows only the white candle of the initiation ceremony. *Credit: Cam Chasteen*

have had subconscious inklings of future events that took shape in her books. These details would come back to haunt her during the months and years following her daughter Kaitlyn's murder. Perhaps Duncan's heritage—her mother was of Irish, Scottish, and Welsh descent—can be credited with her psychic inclinations, as there are those who believe that Celtic ancestry predisposes one to psychic gifts.

Kait, too, may have had precognitive abilities, for she had a professional studio photographer, not her mother, take a portrait of her for her school yearbook, saying, "This is how I want people to remember me." This photograph appears on the dust jacket cover of *Who Killed My Daughter?*

A number of reviewers were critical of *Daughters of Eve,* saying the feminist roles were stereotyped. One of the harshest reviewers, Jan M. Goodman, stated: "The book's deceptive interpretation of feminism plus its dangerous stereotypes make it a harmful distortion of reality." Goodman was also concerned with what she describes as "a suspenseful novel that invalidates legitimate problems by presenting misdirected solutions. . . . The violence of her solutions implies that it may be dangerous to even recognize the issues."[2] She goes on to explain that providing only these extreme solutions in the story implies that Duncan "clearly places a harsh value judgment on [such acts] and because she provides no alternative solutions, she leaves the impression that fighting for women's rights leads to uncontrollable anger and senseless destruction" (Goodman, 18).

Other reviewers commended the book, however. An assessment in *Booklist* concluded that "Duncan has successfully created a disturbing climate of latent evil—couched within the familiarity of teenage life—where vicious acts go unpunished and villains triumph and, as in the past, has manipulated everything for maximum effect."[3]

Another critic, Natalie Babbitt, herself an author of books for young adults, said in the *New York Times Book Review:*

> As Irene's paranoia reveals itself, the reader begins to see that Lois Duncan has . . . chosen the Movement only as a setting and is detached enough to use it with great effectiveness. I was reminded of William Golding's "Lord of the Flies"—the horror of Lois Duncan's novel erupts just as violently at the end. Still, "Daughters of Eve" seems less real than "Lord of the Flies," for all of that work's phantasmagoria. Perhaps this is because the Golding novel is set on a desert island where anything might happen, whereas "Eve" takes places down the street.
>
> What is vivid, though, is the female rage that Lois Duncan portrays—any open-minded reader is bound to recognize much of it—and the story itself is finely constructed and told. Also— how refreshing!—there are no lessons. Instead this novel enables us to see ourselves as the barely civilized creatures we truly are, and it is strongly evenhanded, for it lets us see that women can be as bloodthirsty as men ever were.[4]

Babbitt's assessment seems a fair one. Duncan certainly had not planned the book to be a diatribe against feminism; as a working divorcée with three youngsters to support, she was well aware of the problems of women in the twentieth century. Instead, she had intended the book to be a lesson for young people regarding manipulation. In this case the manipulator was an adult rather than another teen. As such, it is an important book for young adults, because teens are not always as discerning about the motivations of adults as they are about those of people their own age.

Duncan's Writing

In *Chapters* Duncan tells how she uses details from her own life in the fictional books she writes. One such incident occurs in *Daughters of Eve*. Holly Underwood listens to her mother play Debussy on the piano. In this scene Duncan recaptures her own feelings of when she was sixteen and attended a concert of classical music, including Debussy, with a boyfriend. Although Duncan keeps descriptions to a minimum in order to keep the plot moving quickly, the brief bits of detail she does include ring very true because they are based on real feelings and experiences.

It has been noted by a number of people that Duncan is an expert at using cliff-hangers—knowing just when to break off a chapter at a suspenseful moment so the reader will immediately begin the next. She used this technique judiciously in *Daughters of Eve,* for it is primarily the latter chapters of the book which cause the reader to keep going. It is like being in a mental race. As the story builds toward its climax, the reader is forced to continue, becoming nearly breathless in the process. In other words, the pacing is excellent.

Earlier chapters in the novel tend to end on a more reflective, more leisurely note:

> "It's so hot in here," she said weakly. "I think I'd better go out—where it's not so hot." She got up from her seat and crossed the room and opened the door. The air from the hallways felt cool against her face.

"Hey, Tammy, where are you going?" Kelly Johnson called out to her, but she did not answer. Halfway down the hall she broke into a run. She reached the door at the end and hurled herself against it, pushing it wide, and a moment later she was outside, running through the golden sweetness of the September afternoon. (*Daughters*, 31–32)

The last phrase of this action passage gently leads Tammy and the reader to escape in lovely autumnal weather outside the school. A glance at the first sentence of the next chapter shows quickly that the scene has shifted to a different club member, Ann, probably the most mature member of the group. This, then, is a natural stopping—or pausing—place, since the reader is not overwhelmingly compelled to continue reading immediately.

By contrast, compare the ending of chapter twelve:

Ruth Grange heard the siren when she stood on the porch steps, kissing Tom Brummell good night. She stiffened, turning her head to listen.

"A fire engine?" she said.

"Or an ambulance. It's close, isn't it? It sounds as though it's only a couple of blocks away."

"I hate sirens," Ruth said with a shudder. "They give me the creeps."

On his way home, Tom passed the ambulance. It was parked with its lights flashing in front of the Snow house. (*Daughters*, 165)

If readers turn from here to the next chapter, they find that although the scene has changed to another location and other club members, Tom is relating what he has seen, maintaining the plot line without a break in continuity.

Gender Roles

In addition to the issue of feminism, this book contains interesting subtleties regarding parental expectations. The majority of the parents in *Daughters of Eve* want their daughters to have traditional ambitions. They expect the girls to aspire to be wives and mothers. Although higher education is a definite possibility for Fran and Tammy, the other girls in the club are not encouraged by their parents to aim for high-powered careers.

In an article exploring the relationship of the mothers and daughters of the girls in *Daughters of Eve,* Jeanne Gerlach points out that the mothers see their daughters as younger versions of themselves, with similar futures. When Irene Stark enters the scene, however, the girls are able to articulate feelings they were unable to express easily or effectively to their own mothers. Ruthie Grange objects to her unfair treatment as a servant to her brothers, but her parents cow her into submission until Irene suggests a way for Ruthie to handle her problem. As is true of many adolescents, the young women in *Daughters of Eve* find themselves questioning their mothers' roles and their own futures.

As Gerlach points out:

> It is important to note here that educators, researchers, and psychologists have agreed that mothers tend to inhibit in two ways the development in their daughters of a separate self. First, they expect their daughters to remain at home more often than they do their sons. Second, girls are generally expected to help their mothers with "women's work" around the home even after they have started school. The daughter can be shaped into the "little mother" and taught traditional skills of motherhood, including cooking, sewing, cleaning, and nurturing. Mothers, then, often mold daughters into their own images or consciously set out to create daughters who will not repeat their experiences but will live out a life that some ill fate snatched from them.[5]

If one considers the lives of the mothers, it is particularly interesting to compare the brief epilogue about the daughters in this novel. Most of the girls in the story pursue conventional lives and have indeed become like their mothers. To feminists, this is the ultimate irony, for although Irene Stark has managed to be promoted, the girls she has tried to encourage to be more assertive have apparently, for the most part, rejected her ideas. Although we have only the capsule description in the epilogue of what happened later, most of the girls have seemingly continued their lives as if they had never come under the influence of Irene Stark.

7. The Later Thrillers

Although Lois Duncan wrote a number of young adult books with occult themes during the 1970s and 1980s, she continued to formulate straight suspense stories such as *Killing Mr. Griffin*. The books are about teenagers who become involved in scary situations, and their reactions to various kinds of tension as the stories unfold. Duncan is particularly adept at plotting tales of mystery and fright, and these books continue to be popular with teenage readers.

The year before *Down a Dark Hall* was published in 1973, Duncan published *I Know What You Did Last Summer*. It is similar to *Killing Mr. Griffin* in many ways. A group of teens are involved in a deadly situation that had not been intentional, and the selfishness of two members of the group leads them all into lives of guilt and deceit. This book was singled out by the Margaret A. Edwards Award committee, for it "face[s] a universal truth—your actions are important and you are responsible for them."[1]

I Know What You Did Last Summer

One year ago, Julie James was a peppy high school cheerleader involved in many school activities and dating a nice boy, Ray. Now she is a serious, reserved senior, intent on getting admitted to Smith College, her widowed mother's alma mater.

The morning Julie gets her acceptance letter from Smith, she receives an anonymous note that ominously warns, "I know what you did last summer." Julie is chilled by the message, for the previous summer she and Ray and two of their friends had been involved in a hit-and-run accident, killing a ten-year-old boy on a bike. Ray has gone away to California, and Julie has grown apart from the other two friends. After receiving the note, however, she calls the girl involved in the accident, Helen, now a local television personality. They notify the driver of the car that terrible evening, Barry, who is now a freshman at the university in town and is still dating Helen occasionally.

Barry convinces Julie and Helen that the note is unrelated to the accident. In the meantime, Julie acquires a new boyfriend, Bud, a Vietnam veteran, and Ray returns from California. Barry is shot and wounded, ambushed by an unknown sniper. There are more anonymous messages—Helen finds a picture of a child on a bike taped to her door, and Ray receives a newspaper clipping about the hit-and-run incident in the mail. Julie and Ray want to go to the police and confess—they have wanted to from the very beginning—but Helen and Barry remain adamant that their pact of secrecy be honored.

Barry was seriously hurt by the sniper's bullet, and it is thought he may be partially paralyzed, but he eventually recovers. Julie and Ray make contact with the dead boy's family, and learning about the effect the child's death has had on them makes them feel even worse. They discover that the boy has two surviving siblings—an older half sister and half brother.

A man who calls himself Collie moves into Helen's apartment complex and makes friends with her. This is actually Bud, who it turns out is the older half brother of the boy the foursome had killed the summer before. It was Collie/Bud who shot Barry, and now he attempts to kill Helen. Helen escapes, and Collie/Bud goes to the James home, intent on killing Julie. He is prevented from doing so in the nick of time by Ray. He and Julie agree they must tell the police everything.

The story is told primarily from Julie's perspective. As a central character she is sympathetic, although her failure to come forward after the accident is certainly not admirable. It is odd, given Julie's dramatic change in behavior from lively cheerleader to single-minded drudge, that Julie's mother isn't more concerned. She attributes the change in her daughter to Ray's departure—which had been Ray's way of dealing with the situation.

Bud/Collie's malevolence is unfortunately associated with his Vietnam experience. Such stereotyping has been condemned in recent years by Vietnam war veterans and others, and rightly so. Still, in Duncan's hands, the characterization is believable. Bud/Collie is an interesting and complex person, but since the reader is not aware of his dual identity until close to the book's end, it is hard to compare him with the dual-identity characters in Duncan's earlier book, *They Never Came Home.*

It was, in fact, the idea of dual identities that gave Duncan the idea for the book. One evening Duncan was in the kitchen fixing dinner with her daughter, Kerry, and one of her friends. The two girls were gossiping—one about a new boy she had met and liked, the other about an upcoming date. Almost by accident, the two discovered they were talking about the same person. Duncan seized the idea and immediately began to "what if." "*What if* the boy had deliberately implanted himself in the lives of two girls he knew were friends? *What if* he built up a different personality to present to each of them? Why would he do such a thing? What might he hope to accomplish by such deception?" (*How,* 188). She continued this process, saying, "I read an account of a hit and run in the newspaper and got to thinking, what if the driver in an accident decided never to tell, what if someone saw him, what if he decided to tell—and I just kept on what iff-ing."[2]

The two other chief characters in the story, Helen and Barry, are so self-centered the reader may wonder why Ray and Julie were ever friends with them in the first place. Both are concerned primarily with their own images, but even the superficial glamour Helen projects isn't enough to keep Barry interested in her. As a college man, he obviously feels that Helen, a television weather girl (a job that required little education early in the days of that medium), is not his social equal.

It is apparent from the beginning that the accident has made the four culprits uneasy around one another. Their need to forget the terrible night leads them to avoid one another. Yet no one can forget what happened. Barry and Helen tend to rationalize their behavior, while Julie and Ray are consumed with guilt.

The reviews of *I Know What You Did Last Summer* focus on the unlikable characters, yet one describes the book as having "vivid characterization, good balance, and the boding sense of impending danger that adds excitement to the best mystery stories."[3] Duncan's skill as an author has enabled her to create teenage characters who may not be admirable but are realistic. The characters are not necessarily sympathetic, but they may become understandable and sometimes even likable. The reader grows to *care* about what happens to them.

I Know What You Did Last Summer ends on this note:

> "There has been trouble, and it didn't just happen tonight. We want to tell you about it from the very beginning," [Ray said]. . . .
>
> We can never erase it, she [Julie] thought. What we did last summer is done. We can't undo it, ever. But we can face it. That will be something.
>
> Aloud she said, "Why not you, Ray? You were involved as much as the rest of us. Why is it Bud never tried to do anything to you?"
>
> "He did," Ray said softly. "Tonight." His arm tightened around her. "He knew the worst thing for me would be to stay alive in a world without you."[4]

A number of young adult books published after *I Know What You Did Last Summer* are based on a similar premise. One that is interesting to compare is Jay Bennett's *Coverup*, published in 1991. The story is told from the point of view of Brad, a boy who was too drunk to remember for sure what happened one night on the way home from a party. The friend who drove him home, Alden, denies that anything unusual happened, but Brad is bothered by flashbacks that indicate the car had hit someone. Brad meets and falls in love with a girl, Ellen, who is searching for her missing father. In the end, Brad and Ellen help prove that Alden had hit a pedestrian, Ellen's father, and Alden's father has been helping to cover up the incident in order to protect Alden. The plot is a simplified version of typical Duncan plots, with a stronger emphasis on mystery and romance and less on psychological motivation.

The Twisted Window

The Twisted Window is another suspense story by Duncan that is told primarily from the standpoint of the female protagonist. It presents a different type of tale, a mystery in which the heroine gets into a terrifying situation through her own impulsive actions.

Life in Winfield, Texas, doesn't begin to compare with life in New York City for Tracy Lloyd. When Tracy's mother is murdered, Tracy's father, a movie star, decides that Tracy should live with her aunt and uncle in Winfield. Tracy finds it hard to adjust to her new circumstance, and she is resentful of her relatives' attempts to provide a normal, happy home life for her.

One day at school, Tracy is approached by an intriguing boy, Brad Johnson. She knows that there is something not quite right about Brad's story, but she is strongly attracted to him. Also, Tracy is dying to defy her aunt and uncle, and dating this handsome yet suspicious stranger is one way to do that. She discovers he is a liar and confronts him with her information:

> "That's not all you lied about," Tracy continued. "The truth of it is you're not even a student at Winfield. I stopped by the office after school today and asked the secretary to look up your name. There isn't any Brad Johnson in the computer register. The secretary told me this same sort of thing happened before. Last spring there were a couple of young guys who kept hanging around the campus, acting like they were students. It turned out they were dealing drugs they'd smuggled up from Mexico."
>
> "I'm not pushing drugs," Brad said.
>
> "Then what *are* you pushing?"
>
> I'm not pushing anything. It's not like that at all."[5]

Regardless of what she uncovers about Brad, she decides to give him another chance. After a few casual dates, Brad enlists Tracy's help to get his baby sister, Mindy, back from his estranged stepfather, who he tells her has kidnapped the child. Tracy is charmed by Brad and his quest, and she agrees to help him. The stage is set when Tracy finagles a job babysitting Mindy.

Brad arrives later, and the two teens kidnap the child, who insists her name is Cricket. They head out of Winfield toward Albuquerque, New Mexico. Tracy hears on the radio while Brad is asleep that the child they have kidnapped is someone other than Brad's sister. When the three stop for breakfast in New Mexico, Tracy calls Brad's mother from a pay phone and discovers that the real Mindy had been killed four months earlier. When Tracy returns to the restaurant table, she finds Brad and Cricket gone.

Tracy calls her aunt and uncle, who are supportive of her, and finds out that her father is on his way to Winfield from his movie location in Rome. Tracy, however, is determined to undo some of the wrong she has done. She is contacted by Brad's friend, Jamie, and the two decide to head for a mountain cabin where they suspect Brad is hiding out with the kidnapped child. Tracy is surprised to find out that Jamie is a girl; Brad's comments about his friend had made Tracy think Jamie was a boy.

Brad has indeed gone to the cabin in the mountains, where he has dreams of a fantasy family life with "Mindy" and Jamie. In the meantime, however, Jamie tells Tracy about Brad's particular psychological problems, which preceded the death of his half sister. When the two reach the cabin, Tracy sneaks in the back door to get Mindy/Cricket away from her kidnapper, while Jamie distracts Brad out in front. Just as Cricket falls while trying to get to her beloved stuffed animal, the gun Brad is holding goes off. In the monetary shock of seeing the child fall, Brad remembers that he accidentally killed the his sister Mindy by hitting her with his car. Cricket, luckily, is not hurt, and Tracy promises the child she'll take her home to her real mother.

As in *I Know What You Did Last Summer*, certain Duncan touches have been employed to good purpose in this novel, such as relationships with parents, a romantic subplot, and a mystery that keeps the reader guessing throughout most of the book. Here the many mysteries are not caused by inexplicable occurrences; they are represented instead in an allegorical way by an imperfect glass pane—the twisted window of the title—which serves as a symbol for Brad's distorted view of reality. As Sarah Hayes perceptively observes in her review:

> Tracy's changing perceptions of reality affect her view of those around her: her apparently uncaring aunt and uncle are in fact anxious to comfort their troubled niece; her seemingly selfish father is consumed with guilt that his work as an actor allows him no time with his daughter. Appearances are misleading: a sister is not a sister; a kidnapping masks a death; even Brad's best friend, Jamie, turns out to be a girl.
>
> Brad is the only character who stays the same throughout, as the story snakes its way towards the climax, slipping away from the reader just at the point when it seems to become clear. During the final heart-stopping scene in a remote mountain cabin, a shot is fired, a little girl falls to the ground, and Brad is forced, at last, to admit the truth.
>
> Duncan carefully uses her character's shifting views to unsettle the reader.[6]

Zena Sutherland, in her review of the book, comments on the successful use of suspense: "The author deftly builds tension and leads the reader to an expectation (amply fulfilled) of an ending that at first seems surprising—until the reader sees that Duncan has carefully led to its dramatic twist."[7] *Kirkus* also acknowledges Duncan's storytelling prowess. "Duncan is a true pro, grounding the twists of her plotlines with sure motivation and providing the reader with several surprises along the way. Though her writing is undistinguished, it never cheats or disappoints, allowing the reader to believe even this most melodramatic of stories."[8]

Other reviewers wonder how Tracy will deal with her own feelings after she returns to Winfield. But Duncan does not provide pat solutions, and her books do not tell much about what happens later. Even the epilogue to *Daughters of Eve* does not provide all the answers. Simple, brief remarks sum up what happens to the major characters, but there is no lengthy discussion of how the

Left: The cover design for the paperback version of *The Twisted Window*, originally published in 1987. Brad stares through a window, his reflection distorted by the glass as Tracy gasps in surprise and horror. Lower Right: the paperback cover for *Don't Look Behind You,* originally published in 1989, features a slender female hand gripping a telephone receiver as a menacing black gloved hand clasps the wrist.
Credit: Cam Chasteen

characters deal with their feelings and guilt after the story is over. Duncan's purpose is not to neatly anticipate and answer all possible questions; her aim is to tell a fast-moving, exciting story with simple truths. The truth in *The Twisted Window* is Tracy's admission to herself that she has been fooled by Brad and that she must act responsibly to correct a sorry situation. The reader hopes that Tracy has matured enough to deal with all her personal problems, but this cannot be automatically assumed. Growing up is not easy or quick for anyone, and Duncan is an expert at portraying teens as they struggle toward maturity.

Don't Look Behind You

Some critics consider *Don't Look Behind You* Duncan's best teen suspense book to date. Its central character, April, was based on Duncan's daughter Kaitlyn, and the book has been imbued with psychic meaning to Duncan since her daughter's murder.

April Corrigan has a super life. She lives in a nice home in Norwood, Virginia, with her parents and younger brother. She's a local tennis star at her high school and has a handsome boyfriend, Steve. Even her bedroom is special, furnished with antiques provided by her glamorous grandmother, Lorelei. Her friends jokingly call April "Princess."

Then things suddenly change. April's father, a manager for an airline, becomes involved in a drug case, acting as an undercover agent for the FBI. Threatening letters and actual death attempts result in the Corrigans being whisked into hiding and, ultimately, into a federal protection program. April leaves her wonderful life behind, even her dress for the prom, not to mention Steve and all her other friends.

Eventually the Corrigans are provided with new identities, and April becomes Valerie Weber. She is forced to cut off her beautiful blond hair and is given strict orders not to contact anyone from her former life. The family relocates to a small, sleepy town in central Florida. Here April/Valerie is told she cannot even compete in tennis matches, for the family cannot risk discovery.

In loneliness and desperation, April/Valerie acquires a boorish new boyfriend, but dumps him in disgust. She accidentally runs into her old tennis partner from Norwood at Disney World and finds out that Steve is dating another girl. April/Valerie simply cannot stand her awful new life and resolves to recover her old one.

She returns to Norwood, intending to live with her grandmother and finish high school with her old friends. But when she arrives at Lorelei's condominium, she discovers her grandmother has been brutally attacked by Mike Vamp, a hit man hired to kill her father. April/Valerie and her grandmother decide to flee to Florida in Lorelei's Porsche, only to discover they are being followed by the "Vampire" in a black Camaro. In the climactic scene, Valerie kills Mike Vamp by clubbing him with her tennis racket. The family is reunited, though still in danger, and they decide to start a new life elsewhere on their own. An epilogue gives us a brief glimpse of April/Valerie living in a different city, working at a part-time job and maybe finding a new boyfriend. Her attitude about her situation is improved, even positive.

It is interesting to compare *Don't Look Behind You* with Duncan's earlier thrillers. Some of Duncan's favorite themes, such as dual identities, are present. In both *Game of Danger* and *Don't Look Behind You*, the heroines—Anne and April—are forced to cut off their long blond hair to disguise themselves. In both books, the teenage girls are put into dangerous circumstances caused by their fathers' involvement with the FBI. Yet there is a difference in the two stories regarding this last point: in *Game of Danger* no one questions the father's decision to work with the FBI; it is perhaps necessary after the threatened danger to his inlaws. In *Don't Look Behind You*, however, April's father decides to cooperate with the FBI because a friend whom he greatly admires, an FBI agent, asks him to do so. One is almost tempted to compare these two as adult versions of Mark, the manipulator, and Dave, the follower, from *Killing Mr. Griffin*. In most of Duncan's books it is the teenagers who are forced to acknowledge the consequences of their actions; in *Don't Look Behind You* it is April's father who admits he was foolish to let his persuasive friend talk him into doing something that endangers his whole family.

April/Valerie is selfish, yet understandable. Her anger is certainly justified. And she is full of self-confidence; unlike Adam Farmer in Robert Cormier's 1983 novel *I Am the Cheese*, she is never in doubt about who she really is.

In *Who Killed My Daughter?* Duncan describes Kaitlyn, the model for April, and the depiction contributes to our understand-

ing of the fictional character. Kait had that common teenage ail-
ment, a belief in her own invincibility. She was also impulsive, yet
full of kindness. Duncan comments:

> Despite a high level of intelligence, Kait was lacking in judg-
> ment. In *Don't Look Behind You,* there was a scene in which an
> F.B.I. agent snapped at April, "You've still got a lot of growing
> up to do. You're a nice enough kid, but you're part of the Cine-
> max generation. You can't believe real life stories don't always
> have happy endings." I had made that same statement so often
> to Kait that, when she saw it on paper, she burst out laughing.
> "Mother, you're something else! Won't you *ever* lighten up?"
> (*Who,* 35–36)

Reviewers of *Don't Look Behind You* focused on the book's effective use of suspense. Stephanie Zvirin said, "Dialogue may be a bit
stilted . . . but tension escalates nicely. . . . Though April's petu-
lance may grate, her behavior rings true enough, and teens who
relish the trappings of thrillers can immerse themselves in FBI
agents, murder and secrets galore."[9] The critic for *School Library
Journal,* Jeanette Larson, commented, "The entire book is fast-
paced and enthralling, but the conclusion will have readers on the
edge of their chairs.[10]

An interesting feature of *Don't Look Behind You* is Duncan's
use of the witness protection program. It is difficult to find information about this program; obviously, the FBI wants to keep its
methods confidential. When asked about her sources, Duncan
replied that she had relied on a friend, an FBI agent, who was
able to give her some information. He also told her that the program is constantly being changed in order to thwart criminals an-
ticipating FBI action and killing the witnesses.

Don't Look Behind You has been selected by a number of young
readers' choice awards, proving its popularity. However, although
her teen readers enjoy this book very much, Lois Duncan dislikes
it because it seems in a psychic or supernatural way to have
prophesied the murder of her daughter.

8. Who Killed My Daughter?

The summer of 1989 started as a busy one for Lois Duncan. She was contributing articles to *Woman's Day* magazine, and a third book—another young adult thriller—was under contract with her publishers. Duncan was also involved in writing poetry for young children. *Don't Look Behind You* was published in June, and many of her talks and interviews during this time focused on that book, the climax of which is a thrilling chase scene that takes place while the heroine, April, is driving her grandmother to Florida. The car pursuing them is a Camaro. One month after the book's publication, in July 1989, Duncan's daughter was murdered. In Duncan's words:

> It [*Don't Look Behind You*] was published in June [1989]. In July, one month later, Kait was chased down and shot twice in the head by a hit man in a Camaro. Events from my fiction suddenly became hideous reality. In *Don't Look Behind You*, April's family was forced into hiding because of death threats. Two men were indicted for Kait's murder, and since the arrests were made as a result of our family's reward flyers, relatives of the suspected trigger man threatened to kill the rest of us. So our family, like April's, went into hiding and has been that way ever since.

Investigative reporter Mike Gallagher wrote a front page article for our Sunday paper. . . . My character of the boyfriend in
Summer of Fear was named Mike Gallagher. The man indicted
for killing Kait was also named Mike. The police report quoted
an acquaintance of his as saying, "I don't know his last name, his
nickname is Vampires or something—they always called him
'Vamp.'" The hitman in *Don't Look behind You* was named Mike
Vamp. The world in which I lived had turned into "The Twilight
Zone."

As coincidence piled upon coincidence, I began to fear that
grief had driven me mad. (Edwards speech)

She discussed the crime further in a magazine interview:

When the police produced no suspects, our oldest daughter,
Robin, consulted a psychic. Betty Muench told Robin that Kait's
killers had been driving a low-rider; that there were three men,
two in the front seat; and that arrests would be made because
the men would be heard boasting.[1]

A detailed description of the crime appeared in an Albuquerque
newspaper:

Eighteen-year-old Kaitlyn Arquette, an honor student and
daughter of a well-known local children's author, died Monday
night of two gunshot wounds to the head, as her family and police tried to piece together what appeared to be a random, drive-
by shooting.

Kaitlyn was discovered in her car at about 11 P.M. Sunday by
police officers investigating what they thought was a routine car
accident on Lomas near Broadway NE, said Albuquerque police
spokeswoman Mary Molina Mescall.

Mescall said someone apparently had pulled up alongside
Kaitlyn's car as it was moving and fired four gunshots through
the side window. Two bullets struck her head.

"The car went out of control, veered and hit a pole," said Kaitlyn's mother, Lois Arquette.

Kaitlyn, a University of New Mexico student who recently
graduated with honors from Highland High School, had been returning home from dinner with a girlfriend, her mother said.

Kaitlyn died Monday night at about 8:15 at UNM Hospital,
according to a hospital spokeswoman. Police late Monday had no

witnesses, no suspect, no weapon and no explanation for what appeared to be a random shooting, Mescall said. . . .

"I can't imagine anyone doing this deliberately to Kate [sic]," Mrs. Arquette said. "I think it was somebody out having fun with a gun." . . .

Mrs. Arquette said her youngest child was funny, nice and absolutely clean-cut.

"No drugs for Kate. No drinking for Kate," she said.[2]

By the end of that week, the Albuquerque Police Department had some leads. Kaitlyn's memorial service was held on Thursday afternoon. Her family had gathered earlier in Albuquerque, including her brothers, her sister Kerry then living in Dallas with her family, and Robin, working in Florida. Although Kaitlyn never regained consciousness after the shooting, all were able to say goodbye to their sister before she died. In the hospital room a tape of lullabies was played; lullabies written by Kaitlyn's mother and sung by her sister, Robin. After Kaitlyn was declared brain-dead, her vital organs were donated, a desire she had expressed before her death as a result of an article Duncan had written on organ donation.

Another figure at the hospital during those tragic last hours was Dung Ngoc Nguyen, Kaitlyn's Vietnamese boyfriend. He had left Vietnam as a boat person. He and Kait had met at a coffeehouse near the University of New Mexico and had recently moved into an apartment together. At Kaitlyn's memorial service, Nguyen spoke to a reporter:

"I waited and waited and waited for her," Nguyen said. "But she never came home. Nobody called me. Nobody told me nothing."

"Then police came to the door," he said. "They started searching my house, and going through everything. They asked my whereabouts that night. They asked if I had a gun. I kept asking them 'What happened? What happened?'

"When they told me, I went down there, but she had already been taken to the hospital. I went to the hospital. It wasn't like her, it didn't look like her. I didn't know who she was," Nguyen said.[3]

Duncan had accepted her daughter's relationship with Dung Nguyen at face value; she knew Kaitlyn had cared about him a great deal. Following Kait's death, however, Duncan started to hear stories about Nguyen that hinted at a sinister side to the young man. The landlord of Kait's apartment had objected to Nguyen's living there after Kait's death, because he did not like Nguyen, his friends, or his treatment of Kait. Kait's sisters, Kerry and Robin, were suspicious of Nguyen's background and activities. Soon after the memorial service, Nguyen was stabbed in the stomach; he claimed a suicide attempt.

The Albuquerque Police Department continued their investigation of the murder and quickly focused on the theory of a random, drive-by shooting. Two young Mexican men were arrested. The case, however, was hardly airtight, and there were a number of contradictions regarding the movements of the suspects. A former student and friend of Duncan's, Mike Gallagher, then a reporter for the *Albuquerque Journal,* looked into the case. Nearly a year later, he wrote a long article for that paper about the police investigation. In the same issue of the newspaper, another article that Gallagher had written about Dung Nguyen appeared:

The postcard was sent from Albuquerque to the state Attorney General's Office on Feb. 9, 1990.

It read: "Did it ever occur to you that Kait Arquette was murdered as result of a 'hit' order by the Vietnamese mafia? APD refuses to do anything!" . . .

Nguyen, 26, had never been a suspect in the homicide as far as detectives were concerned, although Arquette's girlfriends told police the relationship was marked by bitter arguments.

Within a week of her July 1989 murder, Nguyen attempted to commit suicide. Nguyen told detectives he was depressed over Arquette's death and thought everyone blamed him.

According to police reports, one friend told officers that Arquette had asked her to move into the apartment because she was throwing Nguyen out.

The apartment manager told police shortly after Arquette's death that the couple argued frequently and that she once came to his apartment late at night because she was afraid Nguyen was going to hit her. Arquette also told the apartment manager she was going to force Nguyen to move out.

Police reports show that Arquette's friends also told detectives she had participated in an insurance fraud with Nguyen in a staged car accident during a trip to California.[4]

Nguyen has since disappeared, but Duncan believes he honestly loved Kait and may still come forward with information. She made this belief plain on *Larry King Live*.

KING: OK, where is this boy now?

Ms. DUNCAN: I don't know.

KING: He's not in Albuquerque any more?

Ms. DUNCAN: I have no idea where he is. They let him walk out the door, and I have no idea where he is.

KING: OK. Do you believe he killed your daughter?

Ms. DUNCAN: No, I definitely do not. I think he loved her and I think he was sincerely grief-stricken afterwards. What I think happened was that he introduced Kait to too many things, too many people, told her too much, and she became a threat. And she was executed.

KING: By his friends?

Ms. DUNCAN: I don't even know that that's the case. The police arrested two young Hispanic men later on, and they had some pretty good reason to believe that those men were the trigger men. And then we had a call from a tipster telling us that those men had killed before and did it for pay. So there is a very strong possibility, I would think,

> that, if they did the shooting, it was a
> contract hit. . . . It's going to prove
> that Kait was worth the truth. It
> would be so easy to say, "random
> shooting," and it would have been so
> easy just to keep our mouths shut and
> let Kait go as the golden girl who
> never did anything wrong. But I
> think Kait is worth the truth and
> we're just determined to not let it be
> called a random shooting if it wasn't.[5]

Ultimately, the Mexican suspects were released and charges dropped for lack of evidence. Duncan believes that Robert Schwartz, Albuquerque district attorney, was right to do this, since there wasn't sufficient evidence to convict the suspects. According to a newspaper report, "Both Duncan and Schwartz said they believed the two suspects likely were the gunmen, but they disagreed on whether they were for-hire killers. Duncan said she believes Arquette was killed because she knew too much about an insurance scam run by some Vietnamese in California. Schwartz disagreed with her theory that Arquette's murder was a contract killing. 'I wouldn't hire these guys to mow my lawn, much less mow down a young woman in Albuquerque,' Schwartz said."[6]

In the meantime, however, Duncan had become more aggressive in her attempt to uncover the truth behind her daughter's death.

Any parent, of course, would be shocked and grief-stricken at the death of a child. In Duncan's case, the violent circumstances and unanswered questions gave other dimensions to those well-known stages of grief: shock, denial, outrage, bitterness, and acceptance. In describing the depth of her sorrow, Duncan wrote:

> For months after Kait's death, I was unable to write. When peo-
> ple asked what I did with myself all day, I was honest and told
> them I spent my time grieving. I'd lie on my bed for hours star-
> ing at the ceiling, unable to focus my mind well enough to be pro-
> ductive. Just the shopping and essential housework took all the
> energy I could muster.

Well-meaning friends, concerned about my inactivity, were constantly asking, "When are you going to get back to work?" It was hard to convince them that I was too drained to be creative and that, when the time was right, I'd know it.[7]

Duncan had reacted similarly at an earlier time in her life, "when my mother died the same month that my older daughter was injured in a ski accident, there was no feeling left in me for writing. Months went by, and I was unable to write a thing. I put words on paper but they were lifeless. Everything I produced during that period ended in the wastebasket."[8]

Eventually, Duncan found that she could write through her grief. She wrote primarily poetry in blank verse, departing from the rhyming lines preferred in the past. It dealt with Kaitlyn, of course, and Duncan's feelings about her death. One poignant verse written in February 1990 runs:

> It snowed last night,
> So this morning I went to the cemetery
> To sweep the snow from her grave marker.
> Ice had formed in the letters that spelled her name.
> When I sat on the ice to melt it, she was mortified.
> I heard her voice shriek with the sleek, black crows—
> "Nobody *else's* mother squats in a *graveyard!*" (*Who,* 102)

Duncan started to keep a journal, partly as a record of events, and partly to help bring some sense and order to her thoughts. The final result of this effort was a book published in 1992, *Who Killed My Daughter?*

> When the police investigation fell through and the suspects were released, we decided our only hope to ever get the truth was to make Kait's story public. I had been writing the manuscript all the time to keep myself sane as this thing unfolded. It was Kait's twenty-first birthday last September, and I had three hundred pages of the book. . . . I don't have an ending. Maybe the book will make the ending. So I took the book to the cemetery and plunked it on the grave marker, and I said, "Happy birthday, Honey. This is your present. Mother's going to get your killer." (Edwards speech)

What appeared at first to be two different tracks for Duncan as she pursued Kait's murderer finally merged. The first track involved finding clues about Kait's life. Examining bills, talking with her friends, and even posting flyers around Albuquerque offering a reward for information were some of Duncan's self-imposed tasks. The clues she turned up were shared with the police, but Duncan experienced a growing sense of futility in what seemed to be their unwillingness to pursue any lines of investigation other than their original theory, that of a random, drive-by shooting.

The other activity track was begun with hesitation. Duncan's oldest daughter, Robin, and youngest daughter, Kait, had been especially close. Robin Arquette, more accepting of psychic phenomena than Duncan, visited a psychic named Betty Muench in Albuquerque soon after Kait's murder. As Duncan said, "I'd been annoyed with Robin for going to a psychic. Despite the fact my fiction included psychic characters, I still regarded them as shameless opportunists who took advantage of vulnerable people" ("Who," 34, 36).

Duncan at first seemed to agree with skeptic James Randi, who wrote "'Police psychics' have been investigated scientifically and found to be of no use; in fact, they impede investigations."[9] But Duncan's opinions about psychics changed. She was impressed with Betty Muench's approach. As she explains, "Muench—who usually charges for readings—refused to accept payment from Robin. And many of her statements and predictions proved accurate."[10]

Duncan became less skeptical as she worked with Muench. She became interested in a number of New Age philosophies, and eventually was convinced that she could communicate with her dead daughter, who she believed was on another plane, waiting for certain things to be resolved before moving on to her next level of existence.

In her explorations, Duncan contacted Dr. William Roll, director of the Psychical Research Foundation. He asked Duncan to record her psychic experiences for the association's journal, *Theta*. When Duncan asked him to recommend psychics who might be willing to work with her on solving the murder mystery and as sources for a *Woman's Day* article, Roll suggested that she contact Marcello Truzzi, author of *The Blue Sense*. Roll said that Truzzi personally judged psychics according to high standards, and Duncan could trust any recommendations he might give her.

Duncan had known a boy from Sarasota with the same name, and Truzzi turned out to be this same acquaintance. He was the son of a Ringling Brothers's circus performer. Truzzi recommended other psychics for her to contact, including Noreen Renier and Nancy Czetli, both discussed by Duncan in a piece for *Woman's Day*. These two psychics have worked with police in solving crimes and both treat their abilities as ordinary. As Nancy Czetli states, "I don't think psychic ability is any more mysterious than any other talent—writing, painting, skating or a knack for foreign languages. It frustrates me to see psychics portrayed in the movies because they're all so weird. When people meet me, they're surprised that I'm so disgustingly average. A photographer once said, "Please, do something that looks psychic." I told him, "No, I want people to know that what I do for a living is perfectly normal" (Psychics, 130).

Working with psychics provided Duncan with some ideas and clues, but psychic information is often maddeningly devoid of specifics. One such piece of information hinted at the involvement of an important, though unnamed, state legislator. In spite of this, Betty Muench was helpful to Duncan in easing the grief process and providing insights about Kait before and after her death. Nancy Renier worked with a police artist to create sketches of the perpetrators of the crime, as well as channeling messages from Kait about her movements on the day of the murder. She also provided clues about a "Desert Castle," a place Kaitlyn may have visited on the evening of her shooting. Nancy Czetli and Betty Muench also revealed details about this house, where Kait may well have seen more than she should have, triggering her later execution-style murder. The Mediterranean-style house was located by Duncan in the hills near Albuquerque; although it was furnished, no one seemed to live there.

One of the most intriguing details came from the sketch produced as a result of Nancy Renier's work. While the sketch was being produced, Duncan willed Kait to provide assistance. The final drawing was almost identical to the depiction of the character Mike Vamp on the cover of the British edition of *Don't Look Behind You*. The proposed cover had arrived at Duncan's house just before Kait's murder, and Kait had seen the artwork. Duncan believes Kait influenced Renier's drawing in order to confirm that her murderer, like Mike Vamp, had been a hired killer, a hit man.

Slowly, pieces from various sources started to slide into the puzzle, albeit a jigsaw picture with important pieces missing. The similarity of some of the clues impressed Duncan's husband, a scientist. "'When you give the same problem to three consultants and get the same answer from all three, you have to pay attention,' he said" (Psychics, 50).

Duncan sent photographs of houses in the hills that possibly fit the description of Desert Castle to Nancy Czetli, who had strong reactions to two different shots. These turned out to be of the same house, photographed from different angles. By this time, the police department avoided talking with Duncan about her discoveries, probably writing her off as a grief-stricken parent who had become somewhat unbalanced in her sorrow. Yet clues kept emerging. Some were based on gossip and hearsay, yet eventually a picture of the events surrounding the crime began to emerge.

This may be what happened. On the evening Kait was murdered, she dropped by her parents' house to visit. She left early, saying she was meeting a friend for dinner and that they were going to help decorate another friend's new apartment. Rather than joining this friend, however, Kait met someone, possibly an old boyfriend with whom she had resumed relations, and they drove to the mysterious Desert Castle. A party was in process there, and among the guests were members of a Vietnamese Mafia drug ring. It is possible that Kait recognized someone at the party, someone very powerful, someone intent on keeping any relation with the party guests secret. Kait gave her assurance that she wouldn't disclose what she had seen, and she was able to leave the party and go on to a girlfriend's apartment. On the way home from there, possibly to her parents' house, she was killed, murdered because she knew too much. Duncan thinks Kait had not talked earlier about the insurance scam because she wanted Nguyen to get out of her apartment and her life. Had he been around when she blew the whistle, he might well have been deported to Vietnam and probable death.

Can this story be proven? Not at present. Duncan is hoping that her book will encourage individuals with information to come forward. She also hopes that the FBI will get involved in solving the crime. One way or another, Duncan is determined to find out what happened.

In promoting the book, Duncan has appeared on a number of national television programs. In an episode of *Sightings* in July 1992, she recounted some of the predictions/clues that her psychics have come up with, over a dozen in all. A number of these predictions have already come true.

The original title Duncan had worked with for *Who Killed My Daughter?* was *One to the Wolves*. One psychic-inspired drawing after Kait's murder features a wolf, its neck pulled back by a collar, signifying that the murderer would be "collared" (captured). Some clues have been less symbolic, including the suggestion that the murderers were driving a low-rider car with three people in it. Betty Muench, who made these predictions, also said help in solving the crime would come from the media. Noreen Renier, in addition to providing the sketch of the hit man, also said Kait had gone to a shopping center with a "C" in its name the night of her murder. It is possible that Kait went the Coronado Mall to meet the person who may have driven her to the Desert Castle.

In her Christmas 1992 letter to family and friends, Duncan talks about other national television exposure, including a reference to Kait's story on a CBS evening news program by Connie Chung about automobile insurance scams. A segment about the murder was filmed in November by *Unsolved Mysteries* for airing in 1993. Duncan says:

> They were unable to cast the part of Kait's boyfriend in Albuquerque. There were lots of Vietnamese actors registered at the talent agencies, and when first approached they were thrilled at the possibility of performing on a national television show, but as soon as they heard what the story was, they panicked. Not one Vietnamese actor showed up for auditions, and the part had

to be cast in L.A. This show has a high success rate for flushing out informants. The wheels are in motion, and we believe that the truth will surface.[11]

Duncan tried to be as truthful as possible in telling this story about her family and their tragedy. He publisher had to ask her to flesh out the personality of her husband, for he seemed to be a rather vague, unformed figure. Duncan did this. The family members felt the account of them was accurate, and could not fault it for its veracity.

Who Killed My Daughter? was promoted by the publishers as a true-crime book; the endorsement blurb on the cover was from best-selling true-crime author Ann Rule, author of *The Stranger Beside Me* and *Small Sacrifices*. An early review written by Ilene Cooper comments:

> Like [*sic*] Duncan does for young readers, the account is a page-turner, but it's very different from many of the true-crime books that appear with depressing regularity. For one thing, Duncan's personal involvement makes the telling much more intense, the grief more cutting, but it is the story's mystical aspects that are its obvious source of fascination. Despite the fact that Duncan had written about such phenomena, she was hardly a believer. So what is she to do with coincidences like this: one of the suspects was nicknamed Mike Vamp, the identical name of the hit-man in a recent Duncan book in which the victim was based on her daughter, Kait. Intertwining all the details of Duncan's investigation (which do get a bit hard to follow) are many psychic ribbons that are not easily dismissed.[12]

The reviewer for *School Library Journal* said, "All of the elements of a suspenseful mystery are here—intrigue, turns and twists at every corner, cover-ups, and page-turning action; the sobering fact is that, this time, they're true."[13]

Carolyn Banks, book review columnist for *Crime Beat*, talked about the pathos of three true crime stories, including *Who Killed My Daughter:*

> When is true crime more than true crime? When the person writing is both scrupulously honest and intimately involved.

The cover of *Who Killed My Daughter?* published in 1992. The photograph on the book jacket is the formal studio portrait of Kait taken shortly before she was murdered.
Credit: Cam Chasteen

> Such books are often viewed with suspicion. We hear about them and wonder if the author isn't exploiting the relationship, making private grief a public issue. . . .
> What else lifts these books above run-of-the-mill true crime? I think a strong sense of purpose. In all three cases, authors are compelled to publish their accounts. . . .
> Lois Duncan's *Who Killed My Daughter?* has justice as its aim: "After spending two years investigating Kait's death, our family has managed to accumulate enough information to form a fragmented picture of what may have happened to her, but the jigsaw puzzle still lacks key pieces that could identify her killers. It is my hope that reading Kait's story will motivate potential informants to supply those pieces."
> When is true crime more than true crime? When the reader is moved to tears. [14]

The reviewer for *Library Journal* comments, "This book is especially well written, perhaps because Duncan's writing comes directly from her broken heart and anguished soul."[15]

Because of these events over the past few years, Duncan now is a believer in New Age philosophies such as reincarnation. When asked about her religious background in general, she responded:

> It was Episcopalian. My father later became interested in Christian Science. We were not a heavily church-going family, but when I went to church, I went to the Episcopal church. I just didn't go to church at all that much, but basically I believed in God and leading a good [moral] life. I was just not really into organized religion as such.
> My New Age beliefs do not conflict in any manner with my previous beliefs, they are just another dimension. I have become much more spiritual since Kait's death. . . . I believe each person's religion is a very personal thing, and you explore until you find what works for you, and you can't push that on anyone else. . . .
> I didn't feel comfortable because I didn't want anyone telling me to be a good person. I could accept certain things and not accept others . . . but I guess I didn't worry about it. I figured that eventually I'd find out. [Since Kait's murder] I was exposed to so many things that I didn't know about before, and now I believe in an afterlife which I probably never thought about. . . . At this point, because we feel that we had direct communication with

Kait through the psychics—information that only Kait knows—she must still exist, so now I believe in an afterlife although I certainly can't say what form it will take. . . .

I still believe in God and leading a good life, and I feel reincarnation, which I've come to accept, does not conflict in any way with my belief of an afterlife and the Deity. (CK interview)

Duncan believes that the mystery surrounding her daughter's murder will eventually be solved. When that happens, she plans to write another book, a sequel to *Who Killed My Daughter?*

9. Views and Overview

Lois Duncan has led an eventful life. A prolific author, her books, especially her young adult thrillers, have been honored with many awards. Her personal life has been rich, punctuated with joys and sorrows, including the brutal murder of her youngest child. Her writing has provided her with a lucrative career, with royalties continuing to come in for domestic and foreign editions of her many books still in print. Movie versions of her books are possibilities. In her late fifties, Duncan has no plans to retire; her writing has been an integral part of her life for too long. At present she finds herself unable to write mysteries because of the one she is living herself, but she is working on a number of projects, including a nonfiction book on psychic phenomena for teen readers with Dr. William Roll.

Lois Duncan is a writer with drive. Any author who produces as much as she has works with self-discipline and control. She writes on a word processor after carefully outlining her stories. Duncan once described in some detail how she constructed the plot for *Killing Mr. Griffin*, showing how she builds to climaxes at various points (RDA interview). She explains her narrative method this way: "Although I've been told that some authors start writing with only a general idea in mind and let their stories evolve

116

on their own, I couldn't work that way myself. My books—especially the suspense novels—are tightly plotted and carefully constructed; every sentence in them is there for a reason. Personally, I can't imagine writing a book without knowing exactly how it's going to end. It would be like setting out on a cross-country trip without a roadmap" (DD pamphlet, 2).

Another young adult author, Norma Fox Mazer, once surveyed some of her author colleagues to find out how they write. Duncan responded with, "Writing is the only part of my life that is private and totally my own." Nonetheless, she also talks with her family about her work, sometimes brainstorming with her daughter Kerry, "who is highly creative and has a very good mind for plotting," and also relying on her husband for factual information.[1]

Duncan is certainly not a teenager herself anymore, but she has retained the memories of how adolescence *feels:* the insecurities, the desperate bravado, and the seething uncertainties. She knows how to select themes and ideas important to teenagers.

Duncan learned early in her writing career that she had a special talent for creating books that appeal to young adults. She has often been asked why she specialized in writing for this age group, to which she points to the positive response of teens to her work. She sometimes quotes the following letter from one of her readers, Barbara Scott, which Duncan received after publication of her first book in 1957:

> I just finished reading your book *Debutante Hill*, and this will probably sound stupid to you, since I am just a nobody, but could you possibly add onto the end of it? Say, for instance, until Paul and Lynn get married, and something about the way the debuts turn out, and what happens to Dirk, and make Ernie and Nancy get married too: It does sound impossible, but just for me, please!!! Just one typed paper, please!!! I am so interested in this book, I can't stand for it to be over. I *must* see another part of it. You won't have to send it to Dodd, Mead and Company, just to me. Please! I will be so GRATEFUL!!!!!!![2]

Duncan says, "The years between twelve and twenty—how unbelievably important! These are the molding years, the habit-forming years that will be the basis for all that comes after. It is a time for reading, not for the sake of duty, not for information gained, but for sheer fun. The teen-ager who finds more pleasure in reading a book than in watching a television program is not going to switch his standards ten years from now. He will be an avid reader to the end of his days" ("No Man's," 29).

Duncan has also commented, "The responsibility that accompanies world making [writing fiction] is formidable. For when an author creates a world and invites readers into it, they never walk out the same as when they walked in. This is especially true for those of us who write for young people. We must be constantly aware that the personalities our readers encounter, and the events in which they participate in the world of the mind may have as strong an effect on them as the people and events they experience in everyday life" (Edwards speech).

She continues:

> The choices involved in creating these worlds are personal ones, and each author makes such decisions according to his or her own sense of values. Some create Dick and Jane worlds in which the sun always shines and evil is nonexistent. Those, if nothing else, can be fun to romp in, and such books serve a useful purpose like proving to youngsters that reading can be as entertaining as watching television sitcoms. Other authors create dark worlds filled with pain and injustice. Those books also have value for children who dwell in similar worlds in real life—and sadly, there are many such children—to draw strength that they are not alone with their problems. (Edwards speech)

In her young adult novels, Duncan tells stories that do not necessarily have happy endings. She acknowledges that this has sometimes proved unpopular with her readers. The only real criticism I've gotten from young readers who write to me is when they say, "Why did you make it end like that? Why didn't you make them get married and live happily ever after? Why did you have so-and-so die? And why couldn't it all have come out like it was meant to?' They think happily ever after is what life ought to be and what life in reality is. I did too—when I was their age" (Sutton interview, 23).

The Nemesis of Television

The above quotes from Duncan over a span of thirty years show that she recognized early the rivals for her readers' attention. She has said:

> Probably more than some writers who handled the heavy subject matter, I made a conscious effort to entertain. I was always aware that I was competing with television, and that fiction books today need to utilize many of the elements of television in order to capture and hang on to the reader. Kids are so conditioned to being able to flip that channel if they don't get instant entertainment that I realized that I could lose them early on by starting out in a manner that was difficult for them. I had to pull them into the story quickly and also use a good many television techniques: a lot of dialogue, not too much description, and pace that kept moving along. So I tried to use entertainment techniques to develop a readership that would want to read my books, who wouldn't just drop them and run and turn on the tube. (Sutton interview, 21)

Duncan has also said, "Today's youth has been raised on a diet of television and has become conditioned to expect instant entertainment. Like many of my colleagues, I now find myself forced to use TV techniques to hold my readers' interests" (DD pamphlet, 3).

Duncan explains more about her thinking in connection with a specific book:

> My primary message (I hope) is that reading is fun. Another underlying message, which seems to work into many of my books, is the importance of taking responsibility for one's own actions. My surface goal in writing *The Twisted Window*, for example, was to produce a fast-paced page-turner, exciting enough to lure teenagers away from TV screens. The story has a second level, however. My heroine, Tracy, does something she senses is wrong and is caught in a current of events that sweeps her toward disaster. The subliminal message in this book is, "Don't give in to peer pressure. Stand firm for what you feel at gut level is right." (DD pamphlet, 3)

Themes in Lois Duncan's Work

In her acceptance speech for the Margaret A. Edwards Award, Duncan expanded on the preceding idea: "One prominent message that runs through most of my own books is the importance of taking responsibility for one's own actions. I like to think of the worlds I create as places in which my readers learn to make moral judgements. I try to create sympathetic viewpoint characters so that my readers will be able to relate to them, but those characters are young, inexperienced, and they often make mistakes. They learn from those mistakes, and I hope my readers will also."

Duncan has indeed used the theme of taking personal responsibility for one's own actions a number of times in her books, especially in *Killing Mr. Griffin* and *The Twisted Window*. She tends to combine this theme with the idea of not giving in to peer pressure, as in *I Know What You Did Last Summer*. The concept of manipulation, as practiced by Mark in *Killing Mr. Griffin*, or by adults like Irene Stark in *Daughters of Eve*, has been tied in as well.

These themes are important for teenagers, who tend to believe they are always right and that they are invincible. They are often selfish, too, traits exemplified by April in *Don't Look Behind You*. Duncan is not heavy handed in her approach, however. Instead, she points out the consequences of rash actions and thoughtless risks. She stresses the importance of making responsible decisions and learning to live with conditions that may not be fair but cannot be changed.

By keeping abreast of societal change, Duncan presents a true picture of the world today and the problems faced by many teens. The relationships her teen characters have with their families and friends are realistic. Not all the teen protagonists live in perfect nuclear families. Some live in single-parent homes, some with extended families like that of David Ruggles in *Killing Mr. Griffin*. The teenagers have romances and friendships, some a bit contrived, such as those within the membership of the *Daughters of Eve*, but others more typical, such as April and Sandy in *Don't Look Behind You*.

As in real life, none of the people in Duncan's books are perfect. Some of the parents seem a bit shadowy and a little too virtuous in the early books, like the Kirtlands in *Ransom*, but in the later books parents are portrayed as flawed, like April's mother, who turns to heavy drinking because of her life in hiding. The critics of Duncan's books have sometimes complained of unsympathetic characters, yet the characterization cannot be faulted for being overly romanticized.

In Duncan's own life it is plain that her family is important to her and provides stability and strength. Although never directly pointed out in her books, Duncan's unspoken message is that family sharing is important, and that selfishness is not an admirable quality.

Duncan has been chided for using her writing ability to produce books that are purely entertainment. However, there are morals imbedded in the stories, and the characters generally learn from their mistakes. Those who do not learn, such as Mark in *Killing Mr. Griffin* and Bruce in *Ransom*, are individuals with twisted, dark personalities. Duncan's message for teens in these cases is also worthwhile: learn to recognize these people for what they are. These are people who may well develop into criminals. To follow them is to court personal disaster.

There is support for traditional values in Duncan's books. Some could even be called moralistic, since it is generally made very plain what is right and what is wrong. But Duncan does not involve her characters in the situations that make for "problem novels." She is not primarily concerned with teaching her readers how to deal with physical disabilities, for example, although she has sometimes developed characters like Dexter in *Ransom*, Jeff in *Stranger with My Face*, and Bill in *Promise for Joyce*, who deal with disabilities. These few examples are definitely subplots to the action of the stories, rather than the primary themes themselves. Moral imperfections are definitely more appealing to Duncan as subject matter than physical disabilities. This is perfectly understandable for an author who writes suspense novels.

Duncan's Place as a Writer

Lois Duncan's place in the history and development of young adult fiction has been firmly established. Her work is extremely popular with teen readers and has influenced other writers of young adult fiction. A number of critics have appraised the body of her work for teens, including Karen Stang Hanley in *Twentieth-Century Children's Writers:*

> Duncan has acknowledged that many autobiographical details find their way into her stories, a fact evident in her sure use of considerable detail. Settings are made carefully explicit; by establishing a genuine sense of place, Duncan firmly grounds even her most bizarre tales in reality. Her gift for characterization is quite remarkable: while many of her heroines share similar backgrounds, they are all distinct personalities, never formulaic. In *Daughters of Eve* ten high school girls are introduced in the first several chapters of the book; yet their names and characters are so distinct that even the most casual reader is unlikely to confuse them.
>
> Although many of her characters are truly evil (Lia in *Stranger with My Face,* Mark in *Killing Mr. Griffin*), Duncan rarely concludes a book on a note of prevailing menace. Rather, she seems to believe that family ties, love, and basic morality together defeat the maleficent powers, or at least keep them in abeyance.
>
> Duncan's smooth style bears witness to her long years of practice in the art of storytelling. Calculated pacing and foreshadowing combine to produce nearly excruciating suspense, and the novels are page turners in the best sense of the phrase.[3]

One clue to Duncan's preeminence in the field is the fact that other writers are compared to her.

> The plot from Duncan's 1973 classic, *I Know What You Did Last Summer,* is mimicked by [Christopher] Pike's *Chain Letter* from 1986. In both books a group of teens accidentally kill a person with a vehicle and then are hunted down by someone seeking revenge. Yet Pike's approach to the material is different from Duncan's. First, there are more characters in *Chain Letter,* thus more types/stereotypes. Second, the acts of re-

venge/terror in *Chain Letter* are both more gruesome and humorous. While Duncan has characters being shot, Pike has them waking up in the middle of the night to a room filled with cockroaches. These facts serve as both a warning and a terror element in Duncan's novel, meant to scare both the character and the reader. In Pike's however, they are meant to gross out the reader and not just scare but often humiliate the character. Finally, the tone is radically different. Duncan's book reads like, well, a Lois Duncan book. There is a certain whitebreadness to it—nice innocent kids who find themselves caught up in something. Pike's reads like Stephen King with that same book-as-movie style, lots of big cliffhanger scenes, characters who are not exactly as they seem and are neither innocent nor even likable at times, and layers of building tension. Duncan wrote a mystery you read to find out who done it; Pike wrote a thriller where you are not intrigued by who done it but why and how it is being done.[4]

Jones continues his comparison of other writers, in this case, R. L. Stine, with Duncan:

Another thing that separates them [new thrillers] from mysteries is the whole notion of "the crime." Often the only crime is in the past and the book isn't so much an attempt to solve a mystery as to survive. Unlike Duncan or Joan Lowery Nixon mysteries, there are few sympathic police/detective types. As a matter of fact, adults play a very small role in most of these novels unless they are "The bad guys who did it." Whereas Duncan's books take place in the real world, the thrillers seem to occur in a particular teen world with its own set of rules, symbols and mortality. (Jones, 4)

In spite of the popularity of newer thriller writers, Lois Duncan's books remain favorites with adolescent and preadolescent readers. This can be illustrated by the many children's choice awards Duncan has received, and by small, in-house studies conducted by teachers and librarians. A survey of middle school children in Maryland during 1988–90, for example, showed Duncan as seventh most popular author in 1988–89, and then as the most popular author the following year.[5]

Lois Duncan's place in young adult literature is assured. Her books are popular with teen readers and valued increasingly by teachers and librarians. She is a writer who cares about her readers and treats them with respect. She doesn't scorn their desire for an enjoyable story, yet manages to subtly pass along moral values. Lois Duncan's books take place in the real world, one that young adults know. It is a world that can be harsh and unfair, but one that Duncan portrays as having many redeeming features. Lois Duncan's window into this world is one of truth and courage.

Appendix
YOUNG ADULT BOOK AWARDS

Chapters: My Growth as a Writer. American Library Association Best Books for Young Adults list, 1982; Notable Children's Trade Book in the Field of Social Studies, 1982; cited for Margaret A. Edwards Award, 1992.

Debutante Hill. Dodd, Mead, Seventeenth Summer Literary Award, 1958.

Don't Look Behind You. Jackrabbit Award, 1989; Parents' Choice Awards, 1989; Virginia Young Readers Award, 1992; Young Hoosier Book Award, 1992.

A Gift of Magic. Indiana Young Hoosier Award, 1983.

I Know What You Did Last Summer. Cited for Margaret A. Edwards Award, 1992.

Killing Mr. Griffin. American Library Association Best of the Best Books, 1978; New York Times Best Books for Children List, 1988; runner-up for the California Young Reader Medal; Massachusetts Children's Book Award, 1982; Alabama Young Readers' Choice Award, 1982–83 and 1986–87; Librarians' Best Book List (England), 1986; cited for Margaret A. Edwards Award, 1992.

Locked in Time. Special Award, Mystery Writers of America, 1986; Child Study Association of America Children's Books of the Year, 1986; South Carolina Young Adult Book Award, 1988; Nevada Young Readers' Award, 1988.

Major Andre, Brave Enemy. New Mexico Press Women, Zia Award, 1969.

Ransom. Special Award, Mystery Writers of America, Edgar Allan Poe Award runner-up, 1966, cited for Margaret A. Edwards Award, 1992.

Stranger with My Face. New York Times Best Book for Young Readers, 1981; American Library Association Best of the Best Books, 1981; Ethical Culture School Book Award, 1981; National League of American Pen Women, 1982; New Mexico Press Women, Zia Award, 1983; Massachusetts Children's Book Award, 1983; South Carolina Young

Readers Award, 1984; California Young Reader Medal, 1984; Indiana Young Hoosier Award, 1986; *English Teachers' Journal* and the University of Iowa, a Best Book of the Year, 1981; Florida Sunshine Authors Young Readers Award, 1986; Twenty Titles on Top Teen Read List (England), 1986.

Summer of Fear. Dorothy Canfield Fisher Award, 1978; California Young Reader Medal, 1983; New Mexico Young Reader Award, New Mexico Land of Enchantment Award, 1983; American Library Association Best Books for Young Adults list, 1976; cited for Margaret A. Edwards Award, 1992.

They Never Came Home. Special Award, Mystery Writers of America, Edgar Allan Poe Award runner-up 1969.

The Third Eye. Special Award, Mystery Writers of America, 1985; Child Study Association of America, Children's Books of the Year, 1986; Colorado Blue Spruce Young Adult Book Award, 1987; West Australian Young Readers Award, 1987.

The Twisted Window. Parent's Choice Honor Book, 1987; Edgar Allan Poe Award runner-up, 1988; Outstanding Book of the Year (Iowa), 1988; cited for Margaret A. Edwards Award, 1992.

Who Killed My Daughter? A Best Adult Book for Young Adults, Young Adult Services Library Association/American Library Association (YALSA/ALA), 1992.

Notes

Chapter 1

1. *Chapters: My Growth as a Writer* (Boston: Little, Brown, 1982), 5; hereafter cited in text as *Chapters*.
2. *How to Write and Sell Your Personal Experiences* (Cincinnati, Ohio: Writers' Digest Books, 1979), 4–5; hereafter cited in text as *How*.
3. Personal interview with Anna Vogtritter, 13 March 1992.
4. *Who Killed My Daughter?* (New York: Delacorte, 1992), 147; hereafter cited in text as *Who*.
5. Personal interview with Lois Duncan, 29 June 1992; hereafter cited in text as CK interview.
6. "Home to Mother," *McCall's* 84 (May 1957).
7. "Making the Leap: Small Time to Big Time," *The Writer* 101 (October 1988), 19.
8. *When the Bough Breaks* (New York: Doubleday, 1973), 15; hereafter cited in text as *When*.
9. Griffiths, Therese, "Confessions of a Writer," *New Mexico Magazine* 57 (August 1979), 12.
10. Delacorte, Dell, *Lois Duncan* (New York: Delacorte, Dell, 1989?), 2; hereafter cited in text as DD pamphlet.
11. "Lisa and the Lion." *McCall's* 86 (October 1958), 38–39, 138–42.
12. *The Middle Sister* (New York: Dodd, Mead, 1961), 23.
13. McElmeel, Sharron, "Interview with Lois Duncan," *Mystery Scene* no. 25 (March 1990), 75–76.
14. American Library Association Press Release, "Lois Duncan Named Margaret A. Edwards Award Recipient," January 1992; hereafter cited in text as ALA Press Release.
15. "Margaret A. Edwards Award Acceptance Speech," ALA Conference, San Francisco, 29 June 1992; reprinted in *Journal of Youth Services in Libraries* (Winter 1993); hereafter cited in text as Edwards speech.

Chapter 2

1. *A Promise for Joyce* (New York: Funk and Wagnall, 1959), 30, 47; hereafter cited in text as *Promise.*
2. *The Terrible Tales of Happy Days School* (Boston: Little, Brown, 1983), 11.
3. *Horses of Dreamland* (Boston: Little, Brown, 1987), [3].
4. *Debutante Hill* (New York: Dodd, Mead, 1958), 22.
5. *Love Song for Joyce* (New York: Funk and Wagnall, 1958), 5; hereafter cited in text as *Love Song.*
6. "Lois Duncan," *Something about the Author: Autobiographical Series,* vol. 2 (Detroit: Gale, 1986), 71; hereafter cited in text as SAA:AS.

Chapter 3

1. *Game of Danger* (New York: Dodd, Mead, 1962), 186.
2. Losinski, Julia, "Children's Section," *Library Journal* 87 (15 November 1962), 4278, 4280.
3. "Game of Danger," *Horn Book* 38 (October 1962), 487.
4. "Point of Violence," *Best Sellers* 1 (September 1966), 287.
5. "Point of Violence," *Kirkus* 35 (15 August 1966), 862.
6. "Point of Violence," *New York Times Book Review* (11 December 1966), 69.
7. Cromie, Alice, "Point of Violence," *Books Today* 3 (20 November 1966), 17.
8. *Ransom* (New York: Laurel-Leaf, 1984), 117; hereafter cited in text as *Ransom.*
9. "Dear Author—My Teacher Is Making Me Write This," *English Journal* 76 (February 1987), 27.
10. Campbell, Patty, *Presenting Robert Cormier,* rev. ed. (Boston: Twayne, 1989), 98.
11. Broderick, Dorothy, "Children's Mysteries and Suspense," *New York Times Book Review* (5 June 1966), 42.
12. *They Never Came Home* (New York: Avon Flare, 1982), 162; hereafter cited in text as *They.*
13. Shephard, Richard F., "They Never Came Home," *New York Times Book Review* (8 June 1969), 42; hereafter cited in text as Shephard.

Chapter 4

1. Rhine, J. B., *Extra-Sensory Perception* (Boston: Bruce Humphries, 1935), 31.

2. Keston, Claudia, *Teacher's Guide to Young Adult Mystery/Horror Bestsellers* (New York: Archway Paperbacks/Pocket Books, 1992), 12.

3. *A Gift of Magic* (New York: Archway, 1972), 201.

4. *Down a Dark Hall* (New York: Laurel-Leaf, 1983), 125–26.

5. Levitas, Gloria, "Down a Dark Hall," *New York Times Book Review* (10 November 1974), 10.

6. *Summer of Fear* (New York: Laurel-Leaf, 1977), 28; hereafter cited in text as *Summer*.

7. RDA Enterprises, "A Visit with Lois Duncan" (Albuquerque: RDA, 1985); hereafter cited in text as RDA interview.

8. Moody, Jennifer, "A Difficult Age," *Times Literary Supplement* (27 March 1981), 339.

9. Mitchell, Janet Lee, *Out-of-Body Experiences* (Jefferson, N.D.: McFarland, 1981), 45.

10. *Stranger with My Face* (New York: Laurel-Leaf, 1982), 154–55; hereafter cited in text as *Stranger*.

11. "Stranger with My Face," *Kirkus* 50 (1 January 1982), 11.

12. "Stranger with My Face," *Bulletin of the Center for Children's Books* 35 (April 1982), 146.

13. *The Third Eye* (New York: Laurel-Leaf, 1985), 146–47.

14. Martindall, Elaine, "The Third Eye" *VOYA* 7 (February 1985), 324.

15. *Locked in Time* (New York: Laurel-Leaf, 1985), 200; hereafter cited in text as *Locked*.

16. Hayes, Sarah, "Front-preservers," *Times Literary Supplement* (9 May 1986), 514C.

17. Donelson, Kenneth L. and Alleen Pace Nilsen, *Literature for Today's Young Adults*, 3d ed (New York: Harper Collins, 1989), 165.

Chapter 5

1. Sutton, Roger, "A Conversation with Lois Duncan," *School Library Journal* 38 (June 1992), 22–3; hereafter cited in text as Sutton interview.

2. *Killing Mr. Griffin* (New York: Laurel-Leaf, 1979), 1; hereafter cited in text as *Killing*.

3. Benson, J., "Dear Abby," *Chicago Tribune* (26 February 1992), 5–6.

4. "Diary of a Censored Mother," *Woman's Day* 50 (1 September 1987): 155–56; hereafter cited in text as "Diary."

5. "Schools. Milpitas, California," *Newsletter on Intellectual Freedom* 37 (June 1988), 122; hereafter cited in text as Milpitas.

6. Stevenson, Drew, "Killing Mr. Griffin," *School Library Journal* 24 (May 1978), 86.

7. "Killing Mr. Griffin," *Horn Book* 54 (August 1978), 400–1.

8. Peck, Richard, "Teaching Teacher a Lesson," *New York Times Book Review* (30 April 1978), 54.

Chapter 6

1. *Daughters of Eve* (New York: Laurel-Leaf, 1980), 20; hereafter cited in text as *Daughters*.

2. Goodman, Jan M., "Daughters of Eve," *Bulletin of the Center for Children's Books* 33 (January 1980), 17; hereafter cited in text as Goodman.

3. "Daughters of Eve," *Booklist* 75 (15 July 1979), 1618.

4. Babbitt, Natalie, "Daughters of Eve," *New York Times Book Review* (27 January 1980), 24.

5. Gerlach, Jeanne, "Mother Daughter Relationships in Lois Duncan's *Daughters of Eve*" *The ALAN Review* A60 (Fall 1991), 36.

Chapter 7

1. AASL/YALSA pamphlet, *Imagineer the Future* (Chicago: ALA, 1992), n.p. (folded flyer).

2. Kailer, Pat, " 'Love of Something New' Inspires Author," *Albuquerque Journal* (31 October 1973), 5.

3. "I Know What You Did Last Summer," *Bulletin of the Center for Children's Books* 27 (February 1974), 93.

4. *I Know What You Did Last Summer* (New York: Archway, 1975), 198.

5. *The Twisted Window* (New York: Laurel-Leaf, 1988), 31.

6. Hayes, Sarah, "Fatal Flaws," *Times Literary Supplement* (29 January 1988), 119.

7. Sutherland, Zena, "The Twisted Window," *Bulletin of the Center for Children's Books* 40 (July/August 1987), 205.

8. "The Twisted Window," *Kirkus* 55 (1 June 1987), 855.

9. "Don't Look Behind You," *Booklist* 85 (15 May 1989), 1638.

10. Larson, Jeanette, "Don't Look Behind You," *School Library Journal* 35 (July 1989), 91.

Chapter 8

1. "Who Killed My Daughter?" *Woman's Day* 55 (2 June 1992), 34; hereafter cited in text as "Who."

2. King, Johanna and Glen Rosales, "Teen-Age Driver Dies after Random Shooting," *Albuquerque Journal* (18 July 1989), A1, A3.

3. Rosales, Glen, "Gray VW Sought in Killing: Memorial Service Held for Victim," *Albuquerque Journal* (21 July 1989), A1.

4. Gallagher, Mike, "Police Clear Boyfriend, But Rumors Persist," *Albuquerque Journal* (8 July 1990), A6.

5. *Larry King Live.* Transcript A579 (Denver: Journal Graphics, 1992), 10; hereafter cited in text as King show.

6. Shoup, Steve, "Mother, DA Hope TV Show Will Flush Out Teen's Killer," *Albuquerque Journal* (10 June 1992), D1.

7. "How to Help Your Friends When They Really Need You," *Woman's Day* 53 (2 November 1990), 50.

8. "Breaking the Writer's Block," *The Writer* 82 (March 1969), 17.

9. Randi, James, "Help Stamp Out Absurd Beliefs," *Time* (13 April 1992), 1980.

10. "Can Psychics Solve Crimes?" *Woman's Day* 55 (1 April 1992) 34, 36; hereafter cited in text as Psychics.

11. Duncan, Lois and Don Arquette, Christmas letter to family and friends, December 1992.

12. Cooper, Ilene, "Who Killed My Daughter?" *Booklist* (15 April 1992), 1482.

13. Lynn, Barbara, "Who Killed My Daughter?" *School Library Journal* 38 (August 1992), 190.

14. Banks, Carolyn, "Mortal Thoughts," *Crime Beat* 1 (October 1992), 64–65.

15. Pugh, Belinda J., "Who Killed My Daughter?" *Library Journal* 117 (1 June 1992), 150.

Chapter 9

1. Mazer, Norma Fox, "I Love It! It's Your Best Best!" *English Journal* 75 (February 1986), 28.

2. "The No Man's Land of Teen-age Fiction," *The Writer* 75 (October 1962), 29; hereafter cited in text as "No Man's."

3. Hanley, Karen Stang, "Duncan, Lois," *Twentieth Century Children's Writers*, 2d ed (New York: St. Martin's Press, 1983), 253.

4. Jones, Patrick, "Climbing Pike's Peak: Young Adult Thrillers," *Kliatt* 26 (September 1992), 3; hereafter cited in text as Jones.

5. Isaacs, Kathleen T., "Go Ask Alice: What Middle Schoolers Choose to Read," *The New Advocate* 5 (Spring 1992), 143.

Selected Bibliography

Primary Works

Young Adult Fiction

Debutante Hill. New York: Dodd, Mead, 1958. New York: Pyramid Willow, 1965.

Love Song for Joyce. [Lois Kerry, pseud.]. New York: Funk and Wagnall, 1958.

A Promise for Joyce. [Lois Kerry, pseud.]. New York: Funk and Wagnall, 1959.

The Middle Sister. New York: Dodd, Mead, 1961.

Game of Danger. New York: Dodd, Mead, 1962.

Season of the Two-Heart. New York: Dodd, Mead, 1964.

Ransom. (entitled, *Five Were Missing* when first published in paperback.) New York: Doubleday, 1966. New York: Laurel-Leaf, 1984.

They Never Came Home. New York: Doubleday, 1969. New York: Avon/Flare, 1982.

Peggy. Boston: Little, Brown, 1970.

A Gift of Magic. Boston: Little, Brown, 1971. New York: Archway, 1972. Illustrated by Arvis Stewart.

I Know What You Did Last Summer. Boston: Little, Brown, 1973. New York: Archway, 1975.

Down a Dark Hall. Boston: Little, Brown, 1974. New York: Laurel-Leaf, 1983.

Summer of Fear. Boston: Little, Brown, 1976. New York: Laurel-Leaf, 1977.

Killing Mr. Griffin. Boston: Little, Brown, 1978. New York: Laurel-Leaf, 1979.

Daughters of Eve. Boston: Little, Brown, 1979. New York: Laurel-Leaf, 1980.

Stranger with My Face. Boston: Little, Brown, 1981. New York: Laurel-Leaf, 1982.

132

The Third Eye. (British title: *The Eyes of Karen Connors.*) Boston: Little, Brown, 1984. New York: Laurel-Leaf, 1985.
Locked in Time. Boston: Little, Brown, 1985. New York: Laurel-Leaf, 1985.
The Twisted Window. New York: Delacorte, 1987. New York: Laurel-Leaf, 1988.
Don't Look Behind You. New York: Delacorte, 1989. New York: Laurel-Leaf, 1990.

Young Adult Nonfiction

Major Andre, Brave Enemy. New York: Putnam, 1969. Illustrated by Tram Marwicke.
Chapters: My Growth as a Writer. Boston: Little, Brown, 1982.

Children's Books

The Littlest One in the Family. New York; Dodd, Mead, 1960. Illustrated by Suzanne K. Larsen.
Silly Mother. New York: Dial, 1962. Illustrated by Suzanne K. Larsen.
Giving Away Suzanne. New York: Dodd, Mead, 1963. Illustrated by Leonard Weisgard.
Hotel for Dogs. Boston: Houghton Mifflin, 1971. Illustrated by Leonard Shortall.
Wonder Kid Meets the Evil Lunch Snatcher. Boston: Little, Brown, 1988. Illustrated by Friso Henstra.
The Circus Comes Home. New York: Delacorte, 1993. Illustrated with photographs by Joseph Janney Steinmetz.

Verse

From Spring to Spring. New York: Westminister, 1982. Illustrated with photographs by Lois Duncan.
The Terrible Tales of Happy Days School. Boston: Little, Brown, 1983. Illustrated by Friso Henstra.
Horses of Dreamland. Boston: Little, Brown, 1985. Illustrated by Donna Diamond.
The Birthday Moon. New York: Viking, 1989. Illustrated by Susan Davis.
Songs from Dreamland: Original Lullabies. New York: Knopf, 1989. Illustrated by Kay Chorao.

Adult Fiction and Nonfiction

Point of Violence. New York: Doubleday, 1966.
When the Bough Breaks. New York: Doubleday, 1973. New York: Bantam, 1974.
How to Write and Sell Your Personal Experiences. Cincinnati, OH: Writer's Digest, 1979.
Who Killed My Daughter? New York: Delacorte, 1992.

Audiovisual Sources

Unpublished Interview. San Francisco, Calif., 29 June 1992. (Audiorecording)
Selling Your Personal Experiences in Magazines. Albuquerque, N.M.: RDA, 1987. (Audiocassette)
"Stranger in Our House." (later titled "Summer of Fear" by distributor, HBO Video) NBC (made for television). Director: Wes Craven. Cast: Linda Blair, Carol Lawrence, Lee Purcell, and Macdonald Carey.
A Visit with Lois Duncan. Albuquerque, N.M.: RDA, 1985. (Videotape)

National Television Appearances

"Good Morning America." ABC 1 June 1992.
"Larry King Live." CNN 9 June 1992. Printed transcript A579. Denver: Journal Graphics, 1992.
"Sightings." Fox 7 July 1992.
"Unsolved Mysteries." NBC 27 January 1993.

Articles

"Lois Duncan." In Anne Commire, ed., *Something about the Author: Autobiographical Series,* vol. 2, 67–80. Detroit: Gale, 1986.
"Diary of a Censored Mother." *Woman's Day,* 1 September 1987.
"How to Help Your Friends When They Really Need You." *Woman's Day,* 2 October 1990.
"Can Psychics Solve Crimes?" *Woman's Day,* 1 April 1992.
"Who Killed My Daughter?" *Woman's Day,* 2 June 1992.

Secondary Works

Biographical and Critical Studies: Articles

Hanley, Karen Stang. "Lois Duncan." In D. L. Kirkpatrick, ed., *Twentieth Century Children's Writers*, 252–54. New York: St. Martin's Press, 1983.

"Lois Duncan." In Agnes Garrett and P. McCue, eds., *Authors & Artists for Young Adults*, vol. 4, 81–94. Detroit: Gale, 1986.

"Lois Duncan." *Something About the Author*, vol. 36, 67–72. Detroit: Gale, 1986.

Prescott, Jani. "Lois Duncan." In Anne Evory, ed., *Contemporary Authors: New Revision Series*, vol. 23, 129–31. Detroit: Gale, 1989.

McElmeel, Sharron. "Interview with Lois Duncan." *Mystery Scene* 25 (March 1990): 75–76.

McElmeel, Sharron. "Update: Lois Duncan; Was It Really Fiction?" *Mystery Scene* 37 (n.d.), 67–9.

Jones, Patrick. "Climbing Pike's Peak: Young Adult Thrillers." *Kliatt* (September 1992): 3–4.

Sutton, Roger. "A Conversation with Lois Duncan." *School Library Journal* (1992): 20–24.

Book Reviews

Daughters of Eve

Babbitt, Natalie, "Daughters of Eve." *New York Times Book Review*, 27 January 1980.

"Daughters of Eve." *Booklist*, 15 July 1979.

Gerlach, Jeanne. "Mother Daughter Relationships in Lois Duncan's *Daughters of Eve*." *ALAN Review*, Fall 1991.

Goodman, Jan M. "Daughters of Eve." *Bulletin of the Center for Children's Books*, January 1980.

Don't Look Behind You

"Don't Look Behind You." *Booklist*, 15 May 1989.

Larson, Jeanette. "Don't Look Behind You." *School Library Journal*, July 1989.

Down a Dark Hall

Levitas, Gloria. "Down a Dark Hall." *New York Times Book Review*, 10 November 1974.

Game of Danger

"Game of Danger. *Horn Book*, October 1962.

Losinski, Julia. "Children's Section." *Library Journal,* 15 November 1962.

I Know What You Did Last Summer

"I Know What You Did Last Summer." *Bulletin of the Center for Children's Books,* February 1974.

Killing Mr. Griffin

"Killing Mr. Griffin." *Horn Book,* August 1978.

Peck, Richard. "Teaching Teacher a Lesson." *New York Times Book Review,* 30 April 1978.

Stevenson, Drew. "Killing Mr. Griffin." *School Library Journal,* May 1978.

Locked in Time

Hayes, Sarah. "Front-preservers." *Times Literary Supplement,* 9 May 1986.

Ransom

Broderick, Dorothy. "Children's Mysteries and Suspense." *New York Times Book Review,* 5 June 1966.

Stranger with My Face

"Stranger with My Face." *Bulletin of the Center for Children's Books,* April 1982.

"Stranger with My Face." *Kirkus,* 1 January 1982.

Summer of Fear

Moody, Jennifer. "A Difficult Age." *Times Literary Supplement,* 27 March 1981.

They Never Came Home

Shephard, Richard F. "They Never Came Home." *New York Times Book Review,* 8 June 1969.

The Third Eye

Martindall, Elaine. "The Third Eye." *Voice of Youth Advocates,* February 1985.

The Twisted Window

Hayes, Sarah. "Fatal Flaws." *Times Literary Supplement,* 29 January 1988.

Sutherland, Zena. "The Twisted Window." *Bulletin of the Center for Children's Books,* July/August 1987.

"The Twisted Window." *Kirkus,* 1 June 1987.

Who Killed My Daughter?

Banks, Carolyn. "Mortal Thoughts." *Crime Beat,* October 1992.

Cooper, Ilene. "Who Killed My Daughter?" *Booklist,* 15 April 1992.

Lynn, Barbara, "Who Killed My Daughter?" *School Library Journal,* August 1992.

Pugh, Belinda J. "Who Killed My Daughter?" *Library Journal,* 1 June 1992.

Index

137

The Author

Cosette Kies is currently chair and professor of the Department of Library and Information Studies at Northern Illinois University. In the academic year of 1994–1995 she will become a professor in the College of Education in the same institution. She is the author of numerous articles and books, including *The Occult in the Western World: A Bibliography* (Library Professional Publications/ Shoestring, 1987), *Supernatural Fiction for Teens,* now in a second edition (Libraries Unlimited, 1992), and *Presenting Young Adult Horror Fiction* (Twayne, 1992). She reviewed occult and horror fiction for *Voice of Youth Advocates* for over ten years.

The Editor

Patricia J. Campbell is an author and critic specializing in books for young adults. She has taught adolescent literature at UCLA and was formerly the assistant coordinator of young adult services for the Los Angeles Public Library. Her literary criticism has been published in the *New York Times Book Review* and many other journals. From 1978 to 1988 her column "The YA Perplex," a monthly review of young adult books, appeared in the *Wilson Library Bulletin*. She now writes a review column on the independent press for that magazine, and a column on controversial issues in adolescent literature for *Horn Book*. Campbell is the author of five books, among them *Presenting Robert Cormier*, the first volume in the Twayne Young Adult Author Series. In 1989 she was the recipient of the American Library Association Grolier Award for distinguished achievement with young people and books. A native of Los Angeles, Campbell now lives on an avocado ranch near San Diego, where she and her husband, David Shore, write and publish books on overseas motorhome travel.